Saving the Planet

OTHER NORTON/WORLDWATCH BOOKS

Lester R. Brown et al.

State of the World 1984

State of the World 1985

State of the World 1986

State of the World 1987

State of the World 1988

State of the World 1989

State of the World 1990

State of the World 1991

The World Watch Reader

SAVING THE PLANET

How to Shape an
Environmentally Sustainable
Global Economy

Lester R. Brown
Christopher Flavin
Sandra Postel

The Worldwatch Environmental Alert Series
Linda Starke, Series Editor

W · W · NORTON & COMPANY
NEW YORK   LONDON

First Edition

The text of this book is composed in Plantin with the display set in
Zapf Book Medium.
Composition and Manufacturing by The Haddon Craftsmen Inc.
Book design by Jacques Chazaud

Library of Congress Cataloging-in-Publication Data
Brown, Lester Russell, 1934–
    Saving the planet : how to shape an environmentally sustainable
global economy / Lester R. Brown. Christopher Flavin, Sandra Postel.
      p.   cm.—(The Worldwatch environmental alert series)
    Includes index.
    1. Economic development—Environmental aspects.
2. Environmental policy.   I. Flavin, Christopher.   II. Postel, Sandra.
III. Title.   IV. Series.
HD75.6.B76   1991
363.7'056—dc20   91–24623

ISBN: 0–393–03070–9
ISBN: 0–393–30823–5 (pbk)

W.W. Norton & Company, Inc., 500 Fifth Avenue, New York, N.Y. 10110
W.W. Norton & Company Ltd., 10 Coptic Street, London WC1A 1PU

1 2 3 4 5 6 7 8 9 0

 This book is printed on recycled paper

Contents

Acknowledgments

Any book of this scope depends on the help and support of others behind the scenes, including much of the staff of the Worldwatch Institute. In particular, we turned to Heather Hanford, Marnie Stetson, and Peter Weber for research assistance, each contributing in numerous ways to the gathering and analysis of data and information, as well as fact checking. Our colleagues Alan Durning, Hilary French, and John Young carefully reviewed the manuscript, and their suggestions helped immeasurably in shaping the final product. We are grateful to all three for turning the manuscript around on such short notice.

We also gratefully acknowledge those foundations that supported our research during the course of this project. Contributing directly or indirectly were the Rockefeller Brothers Fund, the Winthrop Rockefeller

Trust, the Geraldine R. Dodge, George Gund, William and Flora Hewlett, W. Alton Jones, John D. and Catherine T. MacArthur, Andrew W. Mellon, Curtis and Edith Munson, Edward John Noble, Public Welfare, Surdna, and Rockefeller foundations, and the United Nations Population Fund. To all the above, we offer our thanks.

Lester R. Brown, Christopher Flavin, and Sandra Postel

Foreword

June 1992 will be a crucial month for the world. Representatives of nearly every country, including numerous heads of state and scores of ministers, will meet in Rio de Janeiro for the United Nations Conference on Environment and Development (UNCED). Also present will be environmental experts and activists of every stripe, and thousands of journalists from around the world. It is for this audience, as well as for our hundreds of thousands of regular readers, that we have written *Saving the Planet*.

The Brazil conference, known as the "Earth Summit," marks the twentieth anniversary of the United Nations Conference on the Human Environment held in Stockholm. It presents a unique opportunity to reverse the downward spiral that has characterized the health of the natural environment and, to a disturbing degree, the human condition, during the past two decades.

On many fronts, from slowing population growth to stabilizing climate, the nineties is the turnaround decade. If we fail to change our ways in these next few years, environmental degradation will lead to economic decline and the two processes could begin feeding on each other.

Ending the appalling conditions of disease and malnutrition in which a fifth of the world's people live is now dependent on environmental reforms as well as economic and social ones. Following on the heels of the widely acclaimed report of the World Commission on Environment and Development, which argued forcefully that economic development and environmental health are linked, the Brazil conference could translate insight into action.

Leaders attending the Earth Summit can have little doubt that the problems confronting them are far greater in scale and scope than those dealt with by the delegates in Stockholm. Although local air pollution was a major issue in 1972, for example, conditions are now worse in most cities—in some, dramatically so. Meanwhile, it has been somewhat overshadowed by more intractable global atmospheric problems such as ozone depletion and global warming.

But the world is also in a better position to do something than it was in Stockholm. For one, the cold war is over, with East and West cooperating for the first time in decades. And the ideological debates between North and South have become less strident, as some rich nations accept responsibility for global environmental problems, and as poor countries understand that their well-being is threatened by environmental decline. In

Rio, they will meet on common ground: the need to forge a worldwide effort to save the planet.

At the center of the Brazil conference is a planned Earth Charter, a document that has been compared by the UNCED Secretary General, Maurice Strong, to a Magna Carta or bill of rights for the planet. In the Charter and parallel Agenda 21 plan of action, the world community has a chance to go beyond the piecemeal policymaking that has marked the first two decades of ecological awareness, and to address the crucial linkages between various issues.

Perhaps for the first time, world leaders can move from responding to disasters to shaping environmentally healthy societies. The environment can then move to the center of economic decision making, where it belongs.

If the existing economic system is not sustainable, what would an environmentally sustainable one look like? This is the question we have addressed in the first half of the book. And while the outline is by necessity rough, some characteristics are clear. Such an economy has a population that is stable and in balance with its natural support systems, an energy system that does not raise the level of greenhouse gases and disrupt the earth's climate, and a level of material demand that neither exceeds the sustainable yield of forests, grasslands, or fisheries nor systematically destroys the other species with which we share the planet.

The extraordinary challenge confronting us is far clearer than it was in Stockholm in 1972. For example, scientists estimate that with a business-as-usual approach, one fifth of all plant and animal species will disappear over the next 20 years. Merely cutting this rate in half will not suffice. It would only postpone the time when collapsing ecosystems lead to a collapse of civilization itself.

The next step is for the world community to articulate a vision of a sustainable society, and for each individual country to develop its own plans for a national economy that can endure. The Earth Summit provides such an opportunity, particularly in the national reports being prepared. Finally, a series of concrete policies are needed, such as those discussed in the second half of the book: carbon taxes on fossil fuels, extensive family planning programs, incentives for reforestation, and the establishment of global environmental restoration funds.

The term sustainable development is widely used throughout the world today, but few understand what it means. What is lacking in the corridors of power is an ecologically defined vision at the United Nations headquarters in New York, at the World Bank in Washington, or in national capitals such as Mexico City or Tokyo. National governments and international development agencies still focus on the environmental assessment of projects rather than the formulation of development strategies that will lead to environmentally sustainable economies.

The focus of the Rio conference, as mandated by the U.N. General Assembly, is admirably comprehensive, but this may also be a limitation. With dozens of substantive issues on the table for discussion, the big picture may be lost. And with parallel efforts under way to prepare major treaties on climate and biodiversity for consideration in Brazil, efforts could become fragmented.

It is unclear at this point whether the Earth Summit will be successful in articulating a bold, pathbreaking vision, or if it will be able to ignite the kind of international institutional reforms and financial transfers to developing countries that are so badly needed. Certainly, it will be an unprecedented test of the world's capacity for collective action on a set of issues that will confront us for decades to come.

The real challenge is to go beyond viewing environmental issues as discrete problems, and begin moving to the basic economic and social reforms that are needed if we are to save the planet. And, indeed, to save ourselves.

This is the first in a new series of books, the Environmental Alert Series, to be produced by the Worldwatch Institute. We see it as an important addition to the stable of Institute publications—the Worldwatch Paper series, started in 1975; the annual *State of the World,* begun in 1984; and *World Watch* magazine, produced since 1988.

The series aims to provide readers with relatively short but incisive and lively books that will assess pressing problems and issues of the day. They will be written by the Institute's experienced research staff. Independent writer/editor Linda Starke will edit each book in the series.

Like *State of the World,* the Environmental Alert Series will be produced in the United States by W.W. Norton, which has published Worldwatch books since the Institute's inception in 1974. We hope the books will be published in all the world's major languages and many others as well, eventually matching the 23 versions in which *State of the World 1991* appeared.

Although this first book takes an exceptionally broad view of the many issues of concern to Worldwatch, future titles will focus on more specific topics. The next two, for example, will consider limits on material consumption and the growing scarcity of water. We hope to provide comprehensive, up-to-date information and fresh insights on a range of pressing topics, with room for a more comprehensive treatment than is possible in our other publications.

Environmental awareness has reached new heights in most countries in the nineties, but the world has a long way to go in raising environmental literacy to the point where the process of reform becomes self-sustaining. We hope that this book will play a small part in that endeavor.

Lester R. Brown
Christopher Flavin
Sandra Postel

Worldwatch Institute
1776 Massachusetts Ave., N.W.
Washington, D.C. 20036

July 1991

Saving the Planet

1

Uncover
the Lifeboats!

Five days after departing from Southampton, England, the Titanic grazed an iceberg in the North Atlantic. The incident passed unnoticed by most passengers—a mere trembling according to one.

Having heard reports of water entering the hold, Captain Edward J. Smith and Mr. Thomas Andrews, a ship designer who was aboard representing the Titanic's builders, went below to conduct an inspection. Upon returning to the bridge, Mr. Andrews made some rapid calculations, then broke the news to the captain: "The ship is doomed; at best you have one and a half hours before she goes down." An immediate order was issued: Uncover the lifeboats!

The Titanic's passengers were not seasoned sailors. The ship was large and reassuring; it had been their home for the better part of a week. Bankers still intent upon returning to their New York offices continued to plan upcoming business deals. Professors returning from sabbatical leaves still mulled over lesson plans. Eventually, many preferred to stay on board rather than disembark on a tiny lifeboat.

Grasp of an altered reality comes slowly, not as much the result of denial as of not comprehending. When the truth could no longer be denied, the passengers exhibited the entire range of human qualities—from bravery and heroism to cowardice. Some panicked or gave up hope entirely. Others achieved comfort by maintaining the status quo: third class passengers were prevented by many crew members from leaving the flooded steerage quarters for the temporary haven of the upper, higher-priced decks.

In the end, reality could not be denied. Early on the morning of April 15, 1912, the Titanic sank with a loss of over 1,500 lives.[1]

As the twentieth century nears a close, the tale of the Titanic comes uncomfortably close to describing the perceptual gap we now face: our inability to comprehend the scale of the ongoing degradation of the planet and how it will affect our future. Few understand the magnitude of the potential tragedy; fewer still have a good idea of what to do about it.

The Titanic's passengers were mainly innocent victims, but the dilemma now facing society is largely of our own making. And for us, there is still hope. But saving planet earth—and its human passengers—will require going beyond the denial of reality that still characterizes many of our political and business leaders. It also hinges on the collective capacity and will to quickly make the transition from perception to policy change, an unprecedented challenge.

The first step—waking up to the dimensions of the world's environmental problems—has in a sense been under way for more than two decades. At the global level, a key milestone was the U.N. Conference on the

Human Environment held in Stockholm in 1972. The 19 years since that meeting have seen the birth of a worldwide environmental movement, the emergence of thousands of grassroots environmental organizations, and the proliferation of environmental laws and regulations in nations around the world.

By the early nineties, as the world headed to another global environmental summit, this time in Rio de Janeiro, major speeches of prime ministers and presidents were incomplete without mention of the environment. Dozens of corporate executives had declared themselves committed environmentalists. And more than 115 nations had established environment agencies or ministries since 1972.[2]

Laws and ministries are one thing. Real environmental progress is another. The two decades since the Stockholm conference have seen only scattered success stories. The Cuyahoga River in Cleveland no longer catches fire, and swimming has resumed in some of the Great Lakes. Air quality has improved in Tokyo and in many northern European cities as well. Soil erosion has slowed on U.S. cropland.

But outside the "post-industrial" north, progress is rarer: some regions of Eastern Europe now face virtual epidemics of environmental disease, misuse of water resources is reducing the agricultural potential of wide sections of south Asia, and soil erosion is undermining the food prospects of much of Africa. Peru's inability to provide clean water for its people became evident when it was struck in 1991 by the world's worst cholera epidemic in decades. In Mexico City, coin-operated oxygen stations are being planned to help people cope with air pollution that has become life-threatening.[3]

At the global level, almost all of the indicators are

negative. Each year now the level of greenhouse gases in the atmosphere reaches a new high, and the ozone layer grows thinner. These fundamental assaults on the atmosphere are caused almost entirely by rich nations that use most of the fossil fuels and ozone-depleting chemicals. Yet the long-term costs will be borne by humanity as a whole. Ozone depletion may cause skin cancer among Andean peasants who never used aerosol spray cans, while global warming could flood the homelands of Bangladeshis who have never used electricity.

Environmental concerns were viewed by many Third World leaders in 1972 as "luxury problems" that only rich nations could afford to deal with. Although this view is still espoused by some, it has a thoroughly unconvincing ring. In the wattle-and-daub villages and urban shantytowns where most of the Third World lives, environmental quality is more than a question of the quality of life; it is often a matter of life or death. In many nations, environmental degradation is now recognized as a key barrier to governments' ability to meet basic needs and sustain living standards.

Yet despite increased awareness, the health of the planet has deteriorated at an unprecedented rate. Since 1972, the world has lost nearly 200 million hectares of trees, an area the size of the United States east of the Mississippi. Deserts have expanded by 120 million hectares, claiming more land than is planted to crops in China and Nigeria combined. The world's farmers lost about 480 million tons of topsoil, roughly equal to that which covers the agricultural land of India and France. And thousands of plant and animal species with which we shared the planet in 1972 no longer exist.[4]

Since the meeting in Stockholm, human numbers have grown by 1.6 billion—the same number of people that inhabited the planet in 1900. Each year now, the annual addition of more than 90 million people is equivalent to the combined populations of Denmark, Finland, the Netherlands, Norway, Sweden, and the United Kingdom. Meanwhile, world economic output, which historically has parallelled demands on the earth's resources, has increased by nearly 75 percent over the same two decades.[5]

Earth Day 1990 chairman Denis Hayes raised the essential paradox when he asked, "How could we have fought so hard, and won so many battles, only to find ourselves now on the verge of losing the war?" Part of the answer lies in the failure to alter the basic patterns of human activity that cause environmental deterioration—from our reproductive behavior to our dependence on fossil fuels. Like the Titanic's passengers, most of whom were unable to grasp the fundamental nature of their predicament, we are still struggling to understand the dimensions of the changes we are causing.[6]

National governments have focused on building water treatment facilities, controlling air pollutants from power plants, cleaning up toxic waste sites, and trying to find new places to put their garbage. While much of this is necessary, such efforts cannot by themselves restore the planet's environmental health. Stabilizing the climate, for example, depends on restructuring national energy policies. Getting the brakes on population growth requires fundamental changes in social values and services. So far, only a handful of countries have undertaken such initiatives.

The still widely held belief that the global economy can continue along the path it has been following stems in part from a narrow economic view of the world. Anyone who regularly reads the financial papers or business

weeklies would conclude that the world is in reasonably
good shape and that long-term economic prospects are
promising. Even the apparent problems—the U.S. budget deficit, Third World debt, and gyrating oil prices—
are considered minor by most economic planners. They
call for marginal course corrections as they pursue business as usual. To the extent that constraints on economic expansion are discussed on the business pages, it
is in terms of inadequate demand growth rather than
limits imposed by the earth's resources.

Lacking an understanding of the carrying capacity of
ecological systems, economic planners are unable to relate demand levels to the health of the natural world. If
they regularly read the leading scientific journals, their
faith might be shaken. Every major indicator shows
deterioration in natural systems.

These different views of the world have their roots in
economics and ecology—disciplines with intellectual
frameworks that contrast starkly. Economic planners
analyze trends in savings, investment, and growth. They
are guided by economic indicators, seeing the future
more or less as an extrapolation of the past, with little
reason to worry about natural constraints on economic
activity. Advancing technology, many economists believe, can push back any limits. Their view prevails in
the worlds of industry and finance, and in national governments and international development agencies.[7]

Ecologists, on the other hand, study the complex and
ever-changing relationships of living things with their
environments. Although the foundations of this view
originate in biology, other fields such as agronomy, hy-
drology, and demography also contribute. For the ecologist, growth is confined by the parameters of the biosphere. While ecosystems are varied and their responses

hard to anticipate, ecologists do know that assaults on a natural system can lead to its collapse—often in ways that are sudden and unpredictable. The more rapid the change, the bigger the impact and the less predictable the result.[8]

These contrasting views are strikingly evident in the indicators used to measure progress. The data cited by economists show remarkable performance. While growth rates eased somewhat during the eighties, the gross world product still expanded nearly 30 percent, reaching $20 trillion in 1990. International trade, another widely used measure of economic progress, expanded by nearly half. Using stock prices as a gauge, the eighties were even better. Investors on the New York Stock Exchange saw the worth of their portfolios surge. An index of 500 widely held U.S. stocks showed values nearly tripling during the decade. Pension funds, mutual funds, and individual investors all benefited. The value of stocks traded on the Tokyo Exchange climbed even more rapidly.[9]

From an economist's perspective, ecological concerns are but a minor subdiscipline of economics—to be "internalized" in economic models and dealt with at the margins of economic planning. But to an ecologist, the economy is a narrow subset of the global ecosystem. Humanity's expanding economic activities cannot be separated from the natural systems and resources from which they ultimately derive, and any activity that undermines the global ecosystem cannot continue indefinitely. Modern societies, even with their technological sophistication, ignore dependence on nature at their own peril.

The health of the planet is ultimately about the health of its people, and from this perspective as well, disturbing trends emerged during the past two decades. Despite soaring economic output, the ranks of the world's poor have increased. Some 1.2 billion people now meet Robert McNamara's 1978 definition of absolute poverty: "a condition of life so limited by malnutrition, illiteracy, disease, squalid surroundings, high infant mortality, and low life expectancy as to be beneath any reasonable definition of human decency."[10]

During the eighties, average incomes fell 10 percent in most of Latin America; in sub-Saharan Africa they were down 20 percent. Economic "development" is simply not occurring in many countries. And even a large portion of the industrial world is no longer moving forward. In the Soviet Union, the economy has entered a state that economists describe as "free fall." Real income dropped 2 percent in 1990 and is projected to be down 10–15 percent in 1991.[11]

The ranks of the poor are concentrated among the rapidly growing populations of sub-Saharan Africa, Latin America, the Middle East, and South Asia. In 1991, some 17 million people in Africa's Horn face imminent threat of famine. Another 13 million in other parts of the continent are also in danger. The growth in Third World jobs has fallen short of population growth, leaving tens of millions unemployed, and hundreds of millions underemployed. Even more people lack access to clean water, adequate health care, and a full and balanced diet.[12]

The failure of the world community to stem the rising tide of world poverty has many roots. Rapid population growth is one, as is the failure of many governments to reform their economic and political systems. Meanwhile, foreign aid donations have stagnated since the mid-eighties, and $1.2 trillion worth of foreign debt has accumulated, sapping financial earnings and undermining the credit-worthiness of low-income countries. The $950 billion spent on the military in 1990 was the biggest drain on resources of all.[13]

The once separate issues of environment and development are now inextricably linked. Environmental degradation is driving a growing number of people into poverty. And poverty itself has become an agent of ecological degradation, as desperate people consume the resource bases on which they depend. Rather than a choice between the alleviation of poverty and the reversal of environmental decline, world leaders now face the reality that neither goal is achievable unless the other is pursued as well.

Lending urgency to both tasks are the persistent warning signs detected by scientists who are now in the role of the men sent below the decks of the Titanic to investigate. By the late eighties, for example, the world's forests were shrinking by an estimated 17 million hectares each year, up from 11 million hectares in 1980. As the need for cropland led to the clearing of forests and as the demand for firewood, lumber, and paper soared, deforestation gained momentum. Some countries, such as Mauritania and Ethiopia, have lost nearly all their tree cover. Others, such as Côte d'Ivoire and Thailand, will have little left by decade's end.[14]

Equally worrisome is the loss of topsoil from wind and water erosion, and the associated degradation of land. Deforestation and overgrazing, both widespread throughout the Third World, have also led to wholesale land degradation. Each year, some 6 million hectares of land are so severely degraded that they lose their productive capacity, becoming wasteland.[15]

Air pollution is a persistent problem in hundreds of

cities and even many rural areas around the world. Breathing the air in Bombay is now equivalent to smoking 10 cigarettes a day. In Mexico City, the air is considered life-threatening, and female diplomats are urged to return home during a pregnancy. In Bangkok, 2 million automobiles and the use of low-grade leaded gasoline have turned the city's air into a soup of 38 different chemicals. One million of the city's residents were treated for respiratory problems in 1990, lead poisoning is now epidemic in Bangkok's children, and lung cancer is three times as common there as in the rest of the country.[16]

Meanwhile, in many parts of the world, air pollution and acid rain are damaging crops and forests. Many of Europe's forests are deteriorating, and in some cases are already dead. In the northeastern United States, the prized sugar maple is experiencing stunted growth, and foresters believe it is gradually being wiped out. Extensive air-pollution-related forest damage has also been identified in China, which recently passed the United States as the world's leading burner of coal—much of it containing high concentrations of acid-producing sulfur.[17]

Despite widespread improvement in water quality in the United States, the Environmental Protection Agency reported in 1988 that groundwater in 39 states contained pesticides. In 1990, the agency recorded some 100,000 violations of its water quality standards. In Poland, at least half the river water is too polluted even for industrial use. Meanwhile, South Korea's Naktong River has fallen victim to the country's headlong industrialization: some 343 factories along its banks illegally discharged toxic wastes in 1990. Recently, thousands became violently ill in the city of Taegu when their household water was contaminated by phenol, a chemical used in processing circuit boards.[18]

The world's worst water quality crisis is in the Soviet Union's Aral Sea basin. There, the accumulation of agricultural pesticides in local water supplies is causing birth defects, miscarriages, kidney damage, and cancer. In some communities near the Aral Sea, rates of esophageal cancer have soared to seven times the national level. This is but one of many instances of health-damaging levels of pollution in the Soviet Union. An estimate for 1987 put the nationwide health costs at 190 billion rubles, a staggering 11 percent of gross national product.[19]

At the global level, the signs of deterioration are even more unsettling—and the processes at work harder to reverse. New atmospheric measurements made in early 1991 by the U.S. National Aeronautics and Space Administration indicate that the earth's protective ozone layer is being depleted at twice the rate scientists had expected—with a stunning loss of 4–5 percent over the United States in 13 years. Scientists believe that as a result, 200,000 additional deaths from skin cancer could occur in the United States alone during the next 50 years.[20]

The figures used as the basis for the international accord to phase out ozone-destroying chlorofluorocarbons (CFCs)—strengthened in mid-1990 to end CFC manufacture by the year 2000—now turn out to have been too conservative, and the timetable may again have to be accelerated. Even if CFC production were stopped immediately, ozone depletion would continue for two to three decades, and it would probably take decades for the upper atmosphere to recover. For the health-conscious, sunbathing may soon have all the appeal that smoking does today.[21]

Other atmospheric changes are also proceeding at an unsettling rate. During the eighties, the amount of carbon pumped into the atmosphere from the burning of fossil fuels climbed to a new high, and it reached nearly 6 billion tons in 1990. The increasing concentration of this and other greenhouse gases, produced largely by industrial nations, is projected by scientists to lead to rapid increases in global average temperatures during the coming decades.[22]

Although it is still too early to detect greenhouse warming conclusively, the eighties was the warmest decade since recordkeeping began more than a century ago. Climate data show that 1990 was the hottest year so far, with snow cover in the northern hemisphere the lightest since the satellite record began in 1970. Just as it typically takes six months after a recession begins before economists have enough data to officially recognize it, so are scientists now trying to confirm a greenhouse warming that may already be under way.[23]

All these changes in the earth's physical condition—at the local, regional, and global levels—are having a devastating effect on the biological diversity of the planet. Although no one knows how many plant and animal species were lost during the eighties, leading biologists estimate that one fifth of the species on earth may disappear during the next two decades. What they cannot estimate is how long such a rate of extinction can continue before ecosystems begin to collapse.[24]

Our economies are engaged in a disguised form of deficit financing: processes such as deforestation and overpumping of groundwater inflate current output at the expense of long-term productivity. In sector after sector, we violate fundamental principles of environmental sustainability. Relying on an incomplete accounting system, one that does not measure the destruction of natural capital associated with gains in economic output, we deplete our productive assets, satisfying our needs today at the expense of our children. As economist Herman Daly puts it, "there is something fundamentally wrong in treating the earth as if it were a business in liquidation."[25]

To extend the analogy, it is as though a vast industrial corporation quietly sold off a few of its factories each year, using an accounting system that did not reflect these sales. As a result, its cash flow would be strong and profits would rise. Stockholders would be pleased with the annual reports, not realizing that the profits were coming at the expense of the corporation's assets. But once all the factories were sold off, corporate officers would have to inform stockholders that their shares were worthless.

To reverse this pattern, industries and governments will need to alter their world views—focusing less on the short-term financial bottom line and more on the long-term sustainability of the economies they invest in. If we do not change our ways, we may find that the lifeboats are rapidly filling up, and that it is too late for many to get aboard. While the rich may congregate on the upper decks and protect themselves for awhile, they too are ultimately threatened.

The effort required to create a sustainable society is more like mobilizing for war than any other human experience. Time itself is the scarcest resource as we begin preparing for the struggle that will unfold in this decade and beyond. Indeed, we have only a few short years to overcome the political, social, and economic impediments to real progress—to lay the foundations for a fundamentally improved society. Once the self-reinforcing trends of environmental degradation and deepening poverty are too deeply established, only a superhuman effort could break the cycle and reverse the trend.

The nineties will be the environmental decade— whether we want it to be or not. Already, it is a lost decade for many ecosystems and people, but it is also a last chance to begin turning things around. In the years immediately ahead environmental issues will continue to force their way onto the agendas of decision makers at all levels. The state of the environment itself will be the driving force. The agents of change will be the growing legions of grassroots organizations, from rubber tappers in the Amazon to scientists in the Ukraine and activist housewives in Japan.

But if the struggle for a sustainable society is to succeed, we must have some vision of what we are aiming for. If not fossil fuels to power society, then what? If forests are no longer to be cleared to grow food, then how is a larger population to be fed? If a throwaway culture leads inevitably to pollution and resource depletion, how can we satisfy our material needs? In sum, if the present path is so obviously unsound, what vision of the future can we use to guide our actions toward a global community that can endure?

That, in essence, is the challenge taken up in Part I of this book—to draw the outlines of a sustainable society, to describe what it would look like and how it would function. Part II tackles the question of how we get there; in particular, it considers the economic reforms needed to bring human activities into harmony with natural systems. And Part III looks at the agents of change in the struggle for a new world.

A sustainable society is one that satisfies its needs without jeopardizing the prospects of future generations. Of course, we can sketch only a rough blueprint of such a society; we make no pretense of being able to predict the future. But just as any technology of flight, no matter how primitive or advanced, must abide by the basic principles of aerodynamics, so must a lasting society satisfy basic ecological principles. At least two preconditions are undeniable: If population growth is not slowed and climate stabilized, there may not be an ecosystem on earth we can save.

With that understanding, and from accumulated experience to date, we can create a thumbnail sketch of a society that lives within its means—one quite different from, and preferable to, today's. In doing so, we assume only existing technologies and foreseeable improvements in them. New technologies will certainly be developed, and some will ease the task ahead. But we need not put our faith in them; the technical means of building an ecologically sound economy already exist.

Rough though this blueprint is, it provides hope for turning the world off the dead-end path it is now so resolutely marching along.

I

The Shape
of a
Sustainable
Economy

2

The Efficiency
Revolution

Moving away from oil and coal as the world's main energy sources is one clear precondition of a sustainable economy. A U.N.-sponsored scientific panel reported in 1990 that continuing heavy reliance on fossil fuels would risk catastrophic changes in climate; a sustainable world economy, therefore, cannot be primarily powered by oil and coal.[1]

The easiest, fastest, and cheapest way to reduce reliance on these fuels is to use energy more efficiently—that is, to do more with less. By using new technologies to make homes more weather-tight, automobiles more economical in their use of fuel, and stoves more efficient, energy needs can be reduced while the growing needs of people are met. Although advancing technology has yielded steady efficiency gains throughout the past century, this process needs to be accelerated if we are to reduce fossil fuel use sufficiently to stabilize the climate.

The best evidence suggests that stabilizing the climate depends on eventually cutting global carbon emissions to about 1 billion tons annually, about one sixth the current level. This is the maximum amount of carbon that scientists believe the world's oceans are capable of absorbing each year; the rest accumulates in the atmosphere, where it warms the climate.[2]

Achieving a stable world climate by late in the next century will require reductions in world carbon emissions beginning almost immediately. Some 23 countries have established goals, ranging from freezing emissions at current levels to cutting them 30 percent. At the Second World Climate Conference, held in Geneva in November 1990, 137 nations agreed to draft a treaty to slow global warming in time for its adoption at the 1992 U.N. Conference in Rio de Janeiro. Although political differences continue to cloud the negotiations, it appears likely that, at a minimum, a score of industrial countries will soon reorient their energy policies to reduce dependence on fossil fuels.[3]

Studies conducted in several countries have found that lowering energy use in buildings, factories, and transportation systems not only reduces carbon emissions but saves more money than it costs. Many rich nations could cut their carbon emissions by as much as 20 percent over the next 15 years. Developing countries can reduce projected emissions by an even greater amount, while strengthening their economies. Indeed, for the Third World, improved energy efficiency is an essential prerequisite to sustainable development.[4]

Achieving such goals would reverse present trends of

increasing emissions and put the world on a path to achieving the long-range goal of far lower emissions worldwide. Fortunately, many of the technologies to bring carbon emissions down are already at hand and cost-effective. No technical breakthroughs are needed, for example, to double automobile fuel economy, triple the efficiency of lighting systems, or cut typical heating and cooling loads by 75 percent. Technologies developed in the decades ahead will allow even greater gains. The bottom line is that a sustainable economy would need to be at least three times as energy-efficient as today's industrial economies typically are.[5]

Within our lifetimes, Thomas Edison's revolutionary incandescent light bulbs may be found only in museums—replaced by a variety of new lighting systems, including halogen and sodium lights. The most important new light source may be compact fluorescent bulbs that, for example, use 18 watts rather than 75 to produce the same amount of light. The new bulbs, already available today, not only reduce consumers' electricity bills, they last over seven times as long. Combined with other new lighting technologies such as improved ballasts and halogen bulbs, and with the use of day-lighting in new buildings, the use of lighting energy can be cut by more than half.[6]

These new technologies are particularly attractive in developing countries, where despite the fact that many homes still depend on kerosene lights, electric lighting accounts for a large fraction of residential power use. In India, for example, some 300 million incandescent bulbs are responsible for nearly one third of the country's peak electrical demand. If India replaced just 20 percent of these with compact fluorescents, it could avoid building 8,000 megawatts of generating capacity, saving $430 million annually by 2000, and significantly cutting the cost of village electrification. This is an example of leapfrogging—going right from kerosene to high-tech. Already, a prototype factory to produce compact fluorescents is being considered near Bombay.[7]

In both industrial and developing nations, homes in the future are likely to be weather-tight and highly insulated, greatly reducing the need for both heating and cooling. Superinsulated homes in the Canadian province of Saskatchewan are already so tightly built that it does not pay to install a furnace; a small electric baseboard heater is more than adequate. Such homes use one third as much energy as modern Swedish homes do, or one tenth the U.S. average. A low-cost, comfortable, energy-saving home appropriate for village use has been developed by the London-based Intermediate Technology Development Group. It is now being tested in Africa.[8]

Inside such homes, people are likely to be using appliances that are on average three to four times as efficient as those in use today. Some of the greatest savings can come in refrigeration—one of the fastest-growing uses of power in developing countries. Commercial models on the market today can reduce electricity use from 1,500 kilowatt-hours per year to 750; others being developed could bring that figure down to 240 kilowatt-hours. Gains nearly as great are possible in air-conditioners, water heaters, and clothes dryers.[9]

Industry will also be shaped by the need to improve efficiency. Steel-making in the future is likely to rely heavily on electric arc furnaces that require half the energy of the open hearth ones of today. Some energy-intensive materials, such as aluminum, may be used only in select applications, replaced in large measure by less energy-intensive synthetics. Vast improvements in the design and maintenance of electric motors could by themselves eliminate the need for hundreds of large power plants around the world.[10]

Cogeneration (the combined production of heat and power) is likely to become widespread. Many factories may generate their own power with biomass, using the waste heat for industrial processes as well as heating and cooling. Such systems are in wide use in some parts of the world already, and can raise total plant efficiency from 50–70 percent to as high as 90 percent. Excess power can be transferred to the electric grid and used by other consumers. In Germany, new micro-cogeneration systems are now being introduced that allow restaurants, apartment buildings, and other facilities to produce power for themselves.[11]

Transportation systems in a sustainable world will almost certainly be far more energy-efficient than they are today. During the past 15 years, automobile fuel economy has more than doubled, and technologies that are even more efficient are now at the prototype stage. (See Table 2–1.) Aerodynamic four-passenger prototypes developed by Toyota and Volvo use numerous advanced technologies and get 98 and 71 miles per gallon respectively; prototype solar-electric commuter cars are capable of an equivalent of nearly 200 miles per gallon, though they are not yet ready for market. Such cars produce much less pollution and have the potential to be far safer than today's models.[12]

Improving energy efficiency will not substantially alter life-styles, though in some cases it may lead to improvements in comfort—and to reductions in energy bills. A highly efficient refrigerator, light bulb, or automobile provides the same service as an inefficient one—just more economically.

Already, a revolution in automotive technology is

TABLE 2-1. *Efficiency of Various Transportation Modes, Current and Projected*

Mode	Number of Passengers Assumed	Energy Intensity
		(Kcal per passenger kilometer traveled)
Average New Car, 1973 (14 mpg)	2	699
Chrysler LeBaron, Avg. New Model, 1990[1]	2	349
Geo Metro, Best Model, 1991	2	177
Advanced Honda Civic, planned, 1992	2	151
Volvo LCP 2000 Prototype	2	138
Toyota AXV Prototype	2	100
Current Light Rail	55	161
Current Intercity Bus	40	120
Current Intercity Rail	80	111
Pedestrian	1	100
Bicycle	1	35

[1]Highway mileage. Composite figure would be lower.

SOURCES: See endnote 12.

under way. Fiat has begun to market electric vehicles, and General Motors' new Impact is scheduled for introduction in 1993. The pressure of governments for cleaner cars is encouraging the development of electric cars and also those fueled by natural gas. The ultimate efficient, clean vehicle could appear soon after the turn of the century—a hydrogen-powered car with a fuel cell and electric motor rather than a conventional engine. It could have better range and performance than today's cars but with virtually no emissions. The challenge is to bring down costs so that such a car is economical.[13]

Gains in energy efficiency alone, however, will not reduce fossil fuel carbon emissions by the needed amount. If the climate is to be stabilized, additional steps must be taken to reshape cities, transportation systems, and industrial patterns, fostering a society that is more efficient in all senses. Although today's mass transit systems are only marginally more efficient than the best automobiles, improved technologies combined with fuller use of public transportation have the potential to make this one of the least resource-intensive ways of moving about. The number of automobiles is therefore likely to fall. Within cities, only efficient and clean cars are likely to be permitted in the future. Families might rent larger vehicles for vacations.

The automobile-based modern era is now only about 40 years old, but with its damaging air pollution and traffic congestion, it does not represent the pinnacle in human social evolution. Although a society in which cars play a minor role may be difficult for some to imagine, it is worth remembering that our grandparents would have had a hard time visualizing today's traffic jams and smog-filled cities. Ultimately, a more efficient society is likely to be less congested and polluted.[14]

The pattern of human settlements, now influenced heavily by cheap oil and the automobile, will inevitably be reshaped. More than half the total energy use in industrial countries is related in some way to spatial structure—the relative location of homes, jobs, and shopping sites—according to Susan Owens, geography professor at Cambridge University. It is this separation of working and living spaces that partially drives the wasteful use of energy.[15]

Although major changes in land use will obviously take time, the early stages of that transition may begin almost immediately. Sprawling suburbs, for example, are almost certain to be supplanted. Not only do detached homes now consume large amounts of energy, suburbs force people to rely on automobiles and waste energy performing the ordinary tasks of daily life.[16]

Energy constraints are therefore likely to lead to more compact communities, where homes and shops are within walking or cycling distance. The typical European or Japanese city today has already taken steps toward such a future. Highly developed rail and bus systems move people efficiently between home and work: in Tokyo only 15 percent of commuters drive cars to the office. European cities are usually three times as dense as American cities. Compact urban designs also facilitate improved public transportation systems. In a sustainable economy, rail travel could replace cars and planes for many shorter trips. Such changes in transportation would reduce energy needs, as well as diminish traffic and pollution.[17]

The bicycle can also play a major role, as it already does in much of Asia as well as in some industrial-country towns and cities. In Amsterdam and communities such as Davis, California, bike path networks have been developed that encourage the widespread use of this efficient transport mode. Also likely to develop rapidly is the concept of bike-and-ride, using the bicycle to reach rail systems that then move commuters rapidly into the center city. There are already twice as many bikes as cars worldwide. In a bicycle-centered transport system, the ratio could easily be 10 to 1.[18]

Telecommunications may substitute for travel. Many people could work at home or in satellite offices, connected to colleagues by electronic lines or fiber optic cables rather than crowded highways. Daily trips to the office could be reduced. Fax messages could limit the need for inefficient overnight delivery services. The saved time would both add to worker productivity and raise the quality of life. Already, some state governments and even private companies are encouraging a transition to the "electronic home office." Computerized delivery services may allow people to shop from home—consuming less time as well as energy.[19]

The Arthur D. Little Company in the United States has estimated that 10–20 percent of the miles logged in commuting, business trips, and shopping could be replaced by telecommunications. This would cut total air pollution by 1.8 million tons annually, and lower fuel consumption by 3.5 billion gallons, while freeing up over 3 billion hours that Americans currently spend on the road. The total savings to the U.S. economy: $23 billion a year.[20]

It also makes sense to construct new buildings so as to capture as much sunlight as possible—for both heat and electricity—and perhaps later include a hydrogen-powered cogenerator producing electricity and hot water in the basement. Passive solar residences can be built as densely as 35–50 dwellings to the hectare. A normal U.S. residential suburb, by contrast, is zoned for no more than 10 homes to the hectare. In many cities, district heating and cooling is an efficient alternative. Already in Denmark, 40 percent of the heating for buildings is provided by such plants.[21]

The potential for improved energy efficiency is particularly great in developing countries, since many have failed in the past to keep up with technological improvements in industrial nations and could catch up rapidly in the future. Efficiency levels can be improved quickly when the numbers of buildings and factories are increasing rapidly, since design changes from the start allow large improvements. To take one example of the gap, Third World power plants consume as much as 44 percent more fuel per kilowatt-hour than those in industrial countries, while transmission and distribution losses are three to four times as high.[22]

In some developing countries investments in energy supply account for more than 40 percent of all public expenditures. A recent study suggested that comprehensive efforts to improve energy efficiency could save the Third World $30 billion annually and eliminate the projected need for 500,000 megawatts of power by 2025. Not only is rapidly growing energy demand no longer synonymous with development, it can actually be a major hindrance to development plans by gobbling up scarce financial resources.[23]

Getting off the debilitating fast track in energy growth requires a new emphasis on policies to encourage energy efficiency, allowing rapid adoption of many of the technologies just described. Growth in Third World energy use is propelled by increases in factories, vehicles, and buildings—just as in industrial countries. But even at the household level, village cooking and lighting systems are substantially less efficient than in more modern homes, and can be upgraded at quite modest costs. Indian energy analyst Amulya Reddy estimates that in his state of Karnataka, an aggressive program to improve energy efficiency could cut the government's projected budget for new power plants in the next decade from $17 billion to $6 billion.[24]

Defenders of the status quo contend that reduced energy consumption will lead to massive layoffs in energy-producing industries. To the contrary, the number of jobs in energy will probably grow, and the skills in demand shift dramatically.

The trend in industrial countries is already away from energy-related jobs. Coal mining employment in the United States fell nearly 40 percent between 1980 and 1988, from 246,000 to 151,000, despite a 14-percent increase in coal production. The number of workers in the nation's oil and gas industry shrank from 715,000 to 528,000 over the same period. One minor exception to this trend is in electric utilities, where the number of employees, primarily service workers, rose 10 percent, to 648,000. Most of this increase, however, has likely been offset by a loss of construction jobs as spending on new power plants declined 40 percent in the eighties.[25]

Employment in coal mining is likely to continue declining as societies seek to limit carbon emissions. Countries such as the United Kingdom and Germany are already on this path, with the number of coal miners falling as automation increases. Even in China, with more than 4 million coal miners, increased automation and worker productivity ensure a leveling off of employment in this part of the energy sector.[26]

There is a way, however, to meet energy needs in the future while creating jobs. (See also Chapter 3.) Studies show that each dollar invested in efficiency improvements generates more jobs than a dollar invested in new energy supplies. A 1979 Council on Economic Priorities report found that investments in energy conservation and solar technologies created twice as many jobs as those in the oil, natural gas, or electric power industries. According to the Council, a dollar spent on energy efficiency at the local level produces four times as many jobs as one invested in a new power plant, mainly because reduced energy bills allow investments in other job-creating businesses. In the move away from a fossil fuel economy, many jobs would be created in home insulation, carpentry, and sheet-metal work.[27]

In a 1985 European Community study of Denmark, France, the United Kingdom, and West Germany, investments in district heating and building insulation, for example, were found to save money and produce more jobs than traditional energy investments. A study in Alaska found that home weatherization created more jobs and personal income per dollar than any other investment looked at, including the construction of hospitals, highways, or hydroelectric projects. Evaluations of existing energy-saving programs in Connecticut and Iowa found that they were less expensive and created more work than energy-supply alternatives such as electric power stations.[28]

As communities invest in energy efficiency, economic benefits will ripple through the economy. An energy plan drafted by city officials in San Jose, California, for instance, would create about 175 jobs during its 10-year span, with an initial city investment of just $645,000. The program includes technical assistance such as energy audits and a home energy rating system. It also includes initiatives to reduce energy use in government buildings, setting an example for the community. The city investment, which would spur nearly $20 million in private spending, is expected to pay for itself in two-and-a-half years as a result of lowered energy bills.[29]

The transition to a sustainable energy system will reshape many aspects of today's societies. The biggest changes will inevitably be in developing countries, which are likely to leapfrog forward to a range of new, energy-efficient technologies, including many that will be used in villages. Agriculture would become less energy-intensive, and many farms would be transformed into producers of both food and energy. The economy as a whole is likely to become more decentralized. While some of the changes can be anticipated, others can only be guessed at.

Overall, however, a sustainable energy economy promises to be far less polluted and not so vulnerable to economic crises generated by political upheavals in the Middle East. And while the energy sources themselves may be more expensive, the energy system as a whole could be far more economical. Greater efficiency will tend to lower energy bills and obviate the need for endless investments in pollution controls. For industrial countries, moving away from heavy dependence on fossil fuels can help ensure continued prosperity. For the Third World, it is a prerequisite to sustainable economic development.

3

Building
a Solar Economy

If carbon emissions are to be reduced enough to stabilize
the climate, the world will have to not only improve
energy efficiency but also develop new energy sources.
Although this goal could in theory be achieved with either nuclear power or renewable energy sources based
on sunlight, the recent worldwide turn away from nuclear power and the rapid progress on renewables provides strong evidence that a solar future is in the making.

The technologies are ready to begin building a world
energy system largely powered by solar resources re-
plenished by incoming sunlight and by geothermal energy. Fossil fuels could be reduced to a marginal role.
Moreover, this is the first major energy transition in
which the entire world will likely be involved. Developing countries have the opportunity to move straight into

the solar age, avoiding the financial and environmental burdens of continued dependence on fossil fuels. The outstanding question is whether governments and industries are ready to build on recent progress and speed up the transition to renewable energy.

The contrast with atomic energy could not be starker. Although nuclear power has been heavily supported by governments and currently provides more energy than many of the renewable energy sources, recent developments suggest that societies are in the process of rejecting nuclear power because of its economic and environmental liabilities. Only about 50 nuclear plants were under construction worldwide in 1991—down from 200 in 1980—and ground has been broken on only nine new ones during the past three years. New nuclear orders have stopped entirely in key countries such as Germany, the Soviet Union, and the United States.[1]

One response to this trend is to try to develop new nuclear technologies that are more economical and less accident-prone, as is being attempted in the United States. No one knows whether such efforts will be successful, but even if they are they would not provide a means of safely storing nuclear wastes. Nor would they alleviate concern about the proliferation of weapons-grade nuclear materials. Trying to prevent this in a plutonium-based economy would require a degree of political control inimical to democracy. Faced with such choices, we expect that societies will find the notion of decentralized, solar-based energy economies far more attractive, and will begin aggressively pursuing their development during the nineties.[2]

In many ways, the solar age is where the coal age was when the steam engine was invented in the eighteenth century. At that time, coal was used to heat homes and smelt iron ore, but the notion of using coal-fired steam engines to power factories had not yet emerged. Yet only a short time later the first railroad starting running, and fossil fuels began to transform the world economy. The late twentieth century could be the dawn of the solar age. Technologies have been developed that allow us to harness the energy of the sun effectively, but they are not yet in widespread use, and their potential impact is barely imagined. When it comes to solar technologies, today's political leaders, still captivated by coal and nuclear power, are akin to the steam engine's eighteenth-century skeptics.

Renewable energy resources are far more abundant than fossil fuels. The U.S. Department of Energy estimates that the annual influx of accessible renewable resources in the United States, for example, is more than 10 times its recoverable reserves of fossil and nuclear fuels. Harnessing these resources will take time, but according to a 1990 study by U.S. government scientific laboratories, sufficient renewable energy resources are available to supply the equivalent of 50–70 percent of current U.S. energy use by the year 2030.[3]

Many find it surprising that renewables—primarily biomass and hydropower—already supply about 20 percent of the world's energy. In certain industrial countries, renewables play a central role: Norway, for example, relies on hydropower and wood for more than half its energy. Biomass alone, principally wood, currently meets 35 percent of developing countries' total energy needs, though often not in a manner that is sustainable in the long term. Indeed, degradation or loss of forests in many areas is threatening the fuel supplies of millions of people.[4]

Steady advances have been made since the mid-seventies in a broad array of new energy technologies that will be needed if the world is to greatly increase its reliance on renewable resources. Many of the machines and processes that could provide energy in a solar economy are now almost economically competitive with fossil fuels. Further cost reductions are expected in the next decade as these technologies continue to improve. (See Table 3–1.) The pace of deployment, however, will be determined by energy prices and government policies. After a period of neglect in the eighties, many governments, responding to environmental concerns, have stepped up their support of new energy technologies, perhaps signaling the beginning of a renewable energy boom.[5]

Direct conversion of solar energy will likely be the

TABLE 3-1. *Costs of Renewable Electricity, 1980 and 1988, With Projections for 2000 and 2030*[1]

Technology	1980	1988	2000	2030
	(1988 cents per kilowatt-hour)			
Wind	32[2]	8	5	3
Geothermal	4	4	4	3
Photovoltaic	339	30	10	4
Solar Thermal	24[3]	8[4]	6[5]	—[6]
Biomass[7]	5	5	—	—

[1]All costs are levelized over the expected life of the technology and are rounded; projected costs assume return to high government R&D levels. [2]1981. [3]1984. [4]1989. [5]1994. [6]Estimates for 2030 have not been determined, primarily due to uncertainty in natural gas prices. [7]Future changes in biomass costs are dependent on feedstock cost.

SOURCE: See endnote 5.

cornerstone of a sustainable world energy system. Not
only is sunshine available in great quantity, it is more
widely distributed than any other energy source. Solar
energy is especially well suited to supplying heat at or
below the boiling point of water (used largely for cooking and heating), which accounts for 30–50 percent of
energy use in industrial countries and even more in the
developing world. A few decades from now, societies
may use the sun to heat their buildings and water and to
cook much of their food.[6]

The sun's rays can be harnessed with minor modifi-
cations in building design or orientation. New buildings
may take advantage of natural heating and cooling to cut
energy use by more than 80 percent. In Israel and Jordan, rooftop solar collectors already provide 25–65 percent of domestic hot water. More than 1 million active
solar heating systems and 250,000 passive solar homes,
which rely on natural flows of warm and cool air, have
been built in the United States. Moreover, advanced
solar collectors can produce water so hot that it can
meet the needs of industry. Inexpensive solar box cookers have also taken hold in many rural areas. As many as
100,000 are in use in India, and scores of villages in
Africa, Asia, and Latin America are testing them.[7]

Solar collectors can also turn the sun's rays into electricity. In one design, large mirrored troughs are used to
reflect the sun's rays onto an oil-filled tube that produces steam for an electricity-generating turbine. One
southern Californian company, Luz International, generates 350 megawatts of power with these collectors and
has contracts to install an additional 320 megawatts.
The newest version of this "solar thermal" system turns
22 percent of incoming sunlight into electricity. Spread
over 750 hectares—less than four square miles—of des-

ert, the collectors produce enough power to satisfy the residential needs of nearly a half-million Californians at a cost that is already competitive with generating costs in many regions.[8]

Future solar thermal technologies are expected to produce electricity even more cheaply. Parabolic dishes follow the sun and focus sunlight onto a single point where a small engine that converts heat to electricity can be mounted, or where the energy can be transferred to a central turbine. Since parabolic dishes are built in moderately sized, standardized units, they allow for generating capacity to be added incrementally as needed.[9]

Photovoltaic or solar cells, which convert sunlight into electricity directly, almost certainly will be ubiquitous in a sustainable society. These small, modular units are already used to power communications satellites and pocket calculators and to provide electricity in remote areas. Indeed, worldwide production of photovoltaic cells has mushroomed from just 3 megawatts in 1980 to nearly 50 megawatts in 1990. (See Figure 3–1.) Within a generation, solar cells could be installed widely on building rooftops and in central generating stations. A Japanese company, Sanyo Electric, has incorporated them into roofing shingles.[10]

During the past two decades, the cost of photovoltaic electricity has fallen 100-fold, from $30 a kilowatt-hour to just 30¢. The forces behind the decline are steady improvement in cell efficiency and manufacturing, as well as a demand that has more than doubled every five years. These cost reductions mean that in more remote rural areas, pumping water with photovoltaics is already often cheaper than using diesel generators. Solar cells are also the least expensive source of electricity for much of the rural Third World; more than 6,000 villages in

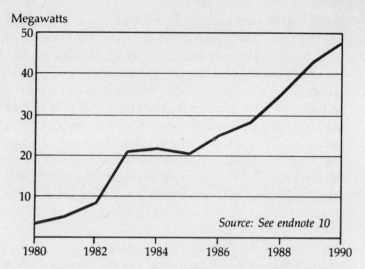

FIGURE 3-1. *World Photovoltaic Shipments, 1980–90*

India now rely on them, and Indonesia and Sri Lanka have initiated ambitious programs.[11]

Photovoltaics, because of their lower projected cost, might eventually take over the central generating role of solar thermal power. By the end of this decade, when solar-cell electricity is expected to cost 10¢ a kilowatt-hour, some countries may turn to photovoltaics to provide power for their nationwide grids. In the more distant future, photovoltaics could provide a large share of the world's electricity—for as little as 4¢ a kilowatt-hour.[12]

Another form of solar energy, wind power, captures the energy that results from the sun's unequal heating of the earth's atmosphere. Electricity is generated by propeller-driven mechanical turbines mounted on towers located in windy regions. By the end of the nineties, the cost of this source of electricity is expected to be around 5¢ a kilowatt-hour. Most of the price reductions have come from experience gained in California, which now has 15,000 wind machines producing 2.5 billion kilowatt-hours annually—enough to meet the needs of all the homes in San Francisco. Denmark, the world's second-largest wind energy producer, received about 2 percent of its power from wind turbines in 1990.[13]

Wind power could provide many countries with one fifth or more of their electricity. Some of the most promising areas are in northern Africa, western China, northern Europe, southern South America, the U.S. western plains, and the trade wind belt around the tropics. A single windy ridge in northern Minnesota could be used to generate three times as much wind power as California gets today.[14]

Living green plants provide yet another means of capturing solar energy. Through photosynthesis, they convert sunlight into biomass that, burned in the form of wood, charcoal, agricultural wastes, or animal dung, is the primary source of energy for nearly half the world— about 2.5 billion people in developing countries. Sub-Saharan Africa derives three quarters of its energy from wood, most of it using inefficient traditional technologies that evolved at a time when wood was abundant. In some areas, this practice is helping to degrade forests, and so the key to sustainable firewood use is tree planting and the use of newer cookstoves that use only a quarter as much wood. The supplementary use of solar cookers in the dry season would also help.[15]

Reliance on bioenergy will undoubtedly increase in the decades ahead, though not as much as some enthusiasts assume. Water shortages, for example, will be a constraint in many areas. And with many forests and

croplands already overstressed, and with food needs
competing for agricultural resources, it is unlikely that
ethanol from corn can supply more than a tiny fraction
of the world's liquid fuels. In the future, ethanol probably will be produced from agricultural and wood wastes
rather than from precious grain. By employing an en-
zymatic process instead of inefficient fermentation, scientists have reduced the cost of wood ethanol from $4 a
gallon to $1.35 over the past 10 years, and expect it to
reach about 60¢ a gallon by the end of the nineties.[16]

More efficient conversion of agricultural and forestry
wastes will allow developing countries to use biomass
energy to meet their growing fuel needs. Methane
derived from agricultural and human wastes already
provides a highly efficient cooking fuel for millions of
people in China and India. For modular electricity generation, highly efficient gas turbines fueled by biomass
can be built even on a very small scale. Some 50,000
megawatts of generating capacity—75 percent of
Africa's 1990 total—could come from burning sugar-
cane residues alone. In the future, integrated agroforestry systems could produce fuel, food, and building materials. (See also Chapter 6.)[17]

Hydropower now supplies nearly a fifth of the world's
electricity. Although there is still ample growth potential, particularly in developing countries, environmental
constraints will greatly limit such development. Small-
scale projects are generally more promising than the
massive ones typically favored by governments and international lending agencies. Smaller dams and reservoirs typically cause less social and ecological disruption. In deciding which hydropower resources to
develop, issues such as land flooding, siltation, and
human displacement will play an important role. These

considerations will probably keep most nations from exploiting all of their potential.[18]

Another important element of a renewable energy system is geothermal energy—the heat of the earth's core. As with biomass, geothermal resources must be carefully tapped and managed if they are to be truly renewable. In this case, mismanagement can lead to depletion of the local heat source. Since geothermal plants can produce power more than 90 percent of the time, they can provide electricity when there is no sun or wind.

Geothermal resources are localized, though found in many regions. Worldwide, more than 5,600 megawatts' worth of geothermal power plants have been built. El Salvador gets 40 percent of its electricity from the earth's natural heat, Nicaragua 28 percent, and Kenya, 11. Most Pacific Rim countries, as well as those along East Africa's Great Rift Valley and around the Mediterranean, could tap geothermal energy. A good deal of Japan, for example, lies over an enormous heat source that could meet much of its energy needs.[19]

While fossil fuels have been in storage for millions of years, renewable energy varies with the weather, the season, and the daily cycle between night and day. Indeed, geothermal, biomass, and hydropower are the only forms that can be stored easily. Although not a constraint initially, the intermittent nature of sunshine and wind means that the large-scale use of renewables will need to be backed by new means of energy storage and transportation.

Using inexpensive solar or wind electricity to produce hydrogen via the electrolysis of water provides a means both of storing solar energy and of transporting it efficiently thousands of kilometers from the deserts or windy plains where it is harnessed. Hydrogen is a clean-burning gaseous fuel that is easier and cheaper to move than oil, coal, or electricity. Moreover, hydrogen can provide the large amounts of concentrated energy needed by today's factories, homes, and transportation systems. It can be used, for example, to run automobiles using either an internal combustion engine or, more efficiently, a fuel cell.[20]

The solar/hydrogen combination could become the cornerstone of a new global energy economy based on renewable resources. All the world's major population concentrations are located within reach of sunny and wind-rich areas. The U.S. Southwest, for example, could supply much of the country with either electricity or hydrogen fuel. The pipelines that link the gas fields in Texas and Oklahoma with the industrial Midwest and the Northeast could carry hydrogen to these regions. While it is true that renewable energy sources are regionally concentrated, they are far less so than oil, where two thirds of proven world reserves are in the Persian Gulf area.[21]

For Europe, solar power plants could be built in southern Spain or in North Africa. From the latter, hydrogen could be transported into Spain at Gibraltar or into Italy via Sicily, following existing natural gas pipelines. Within Europe, today's pipeline and electrical grids make it relatively easy to distribute solar energy. To the east, Kazakhstan and the other semiarid Asian republics could supply much of the Soviet Union's energy. For India, the sun-drenched Thar Desert in the northwest is within easy range of the rest of the country. For China's 1.1 billion people, solar electricity could be generated in the country's vast central and northwestern desert regions.

Although some countries are likely to import renewable energy, the enormous oil-related bills that characterize modern trade relationships will dwindle in a solar economy. And renewable energy sources are to a large extent inflation-proof. Decentralization may be another hallmark of the emerging new energy system. In contrast to today's huge refineries and power plants, renewable electricity sources—whether photovoltaic cells or wood-fired plants—can be developed in various sizes. Solar, wind, and cogeneration facilities can be built at less than one one-thousandth the size of a typical nuclear- or coal-fired plant. Some can even be installed at the household level, and transmission and distribution losses can be minimized.[22]

Even larger-scale renewable energy projects, such as commercial wind farms, are more modular than current energy sources. Wind farms are typically composed of 100-kilowatt turbines that are less than 20 meters in diameter and cost roughly $100,000 to build and install. The manufacturing processes are more akin to today's automobile factories than to central power plants. A wind-power developer can install 10, 100, or 1,000 machines, depending on how much power is needed. The same machine could also be used by itself to supply power for a Third World village.[23]

Areas where renewable sources are abundant and the need for energy great will likely see the arrival of a range of new technologies. Solar thermal power systems may be deployed extensively in deserts, while wind turbines could proliferate in windy regions. Photovoltaics can be used virtually everywhere. No matter the energy technology, however, environmental and land use considerations need careful attention. Although many areas will remain off-limits for renewable energy production due to environmental concerns, this will not substantially hinder renewable energy development.

New solar electric technologies are no more land-intensive than some of today's power sources. In fact, if the land devoted to mining coal is included, most renewable systems actually require less space than coal-fired power plants do. (See Table 3–2.) In coal-rich areas of Eastern Europe, the United States, and India, for example, vast strip mines—gashes in the earth's surface—render large areas useless for generations. Solar technologies, in contrast, need not be spread over wide swaths of land. Photovoltaics can be deployed on rooftops. And while wind farms appear to use large tracts, only 10 percent of the land is occupied by turbine towers and service roads; the remainder can be used for agriculture.[24]

Researchers at the Electric Power Research Institute in California found that 25 percent of today's U.S. elec-

TABLE 3-2. *Land Use of Selected Electricity-Generating Technologies, United States*

Technology	Land Occupied
	(square meters per gigawatt-hour, for 30 years)
Coal[1]	3,642
Solar Thermal	3,561
Photovoltaics	3,237
Wind[2]	1,335
Geothermal	404

[1]Includes coal mining.   [2]Land actually occupied by turbines and service roads.

SOURCE: See endnote 24.

tricity needs could be met by solar cells deployed over an area of 15,000 square kilometers—slightly larger than the state of Connecticut or less than 8 percent of the area used by the U.S. military. Another one quarter of current U.S. generating capacity could be provided by wind farms installed on the windiest 1.5 percent of the continental United States. Most of this is western grazing land that would hardly be affected by wind farm development.[25]

While it takes nearly one hectare of corn to provide enough ethanol to run a U.S. automobile for a year, the same amount of land devoted to solar thermal troughs could power more than 80 electric vehicles, due to the higher conversion efficiency. Moreover, solar technologies can be placed on less valuable land. A hectare of Wyoming scrubland is worth around $100, while a hectare of Iowa farmland costs more than $3,000. A single hectare of inexpensive grazing land in the U.S. high plains could yield more than $25,000 worth of wind-generated electricity annually.[26]

Still, no single energy source can provide all the world's energy. Rather, a range of renewable technologies will likely be deployed. Within a few decades, for example, the United States might get 30 percent of its electricity from sunshine, 20 percent from hydropower, 20 percent from windpower, 10 percent from biomass, 10 percent from geothermal energy, and 10 percent from natural-gas-fired cogeneration—cutting national carbon emissions by more than a third. A north African country may get half its electricity from solar power, while Scandinavia will likley rely on wind, wood, and water power, and the Philippines, on geothermal energy.

The shift to solar energy could also give a boost to the

job market. For a given amount of energy, solar power systems employ more workers than fossil fuel and nuclear power plants do, even when coal mining is included. (See Table 3–3.) One recent study found that New Brunswick, Canada, would create more income and jobs by increasing wood use over the next 20 years than by developing either oil or coal. Wind prospectors, photovoltaic engineers, and solar architects are among the professions emerging. Numbering in the thousands today, such jobs may reach the millions in a few decades.[27]

No completely new technologies are needed to transform the fossil-fuel-based global energy economy to one that is solar-based—only modest, achievable advances in those already in use or under development. Unlike nuclear power plants, each of which takes 6–10 years to build, renewable energy technologies are generally small and modular. Eighty-megawatt solar thermal plants are routinely built in six to eight months. As a result, new

TABLE 3-3. *Direct Employment in Electricity Generation, Various Technologies, United States*

Technology	Jobs
	(per thousand gigawatt-hours a year)
Nuclear	100
Geothermal	112
Coal[1]	116
Solar Thermal	248
Wind	542

[1]Includes coal mining.

SOURCE: See endnote 27.

technologies can evolve rapidly in a single decade. New nuclear technologies, in comparison, would take a minimum of two decades to commercialize.[28]

The shape of a renewable energy system is beginning to emerge. What stands out is the enormous abundance and versatility of the available resources. It seems certain that the mix of technologies used in a solar economy will be diverse; the energy sources harnessed would vary with the climate and natural resources of each region. But almost everywhere, an economy based on renewable energy would be stronger, more stable, and less polluted than today's oil-based economy. For developing countries in particular, a solar future is the only way out of the economic and environmental bind that fossil fuels have put them in.

4

Reusing and Recycling Materials

The throwaway society that has emerged in western societies during the late twentieth century uses so much energy, emits so much carbon, and generates so much air pollution, acid rain, water pollution, toxic waste, and rubbish that it is strangling itself. Rooted in the industrial concept of planned obsolescence and appeals to convenience at almost any cost, it may be seen by historians as an economic aberration. In an environmentally sustainable economy, waste reduction and recycling industries will replace the garbage collection and disposal companies of today.

In such an economy, materials use will be guided by a hierarchy of options. The first priority, of course, is to avoid using any nonessential item. Second is to directly reuse a product—for example, refilling a glass beverage container. The third is to recycle the material to form a new product. Fourth, the material can be burned to extract whatever energy it contains, as long as this can be done safely. The option of last resort is disposal in a landfill.

Most materials used today are discarded after one use—roughly two thirds of all aluminum, three fourths of all steel and paper, and an even higher share of plastic. Society will become dramatically less energy-intensive and less polluting only if the throwaway economy is replaced by one that reuses and recycles. Steel produced entirely from scrap requires only one third as much energy as that produced from iron ore. Newsprint from recycled paper takes 25–60 percent less energy to make than that from virgin wood pulp. And recycling glass saves up to a third of the energy embodied in the original product.[1]

Reuse brings even more dramatic gains. For example, replacing a throwaway beverage bottle with one made from recycled glass reduces energy use by roughly a third, but replacing it with a refillable glass bottle can cut energy use by nine tenths. Although the relative energy savings from reusing versus recycling vary from product to product, these numbers reflect the environmental advantages of reuse.[2]

Recycling is also a key to reducing land, air, and water pollution. For example, steel produced from scrap reduces air pollution by 85 percent, cuts water pollution by 76 percent, and eliminates mining wastes altogether. Making paper from recycled material reduces pollutants entering the air by 74 percent and the water by 35 percent, as well as lowering pressures on forests in direct proportion to the amount recycled.[3]

Although the focus in recent years has been on wastes

at the consumer end of the production cycle, far more is wasted in the mining and processing of both materials and fossil fuels. For example, nonfuel mining in the United States produces, at conservative estimates, 1 billion tons per year of waste material in the form of slag, mine tailings, and other discarded materials—at least six times as much as the garbage produced by U.S. municipalities in 1988.[4]

With most minerals now being produced from surface mines rather than from underground, the land disruption is extensive. A worldwide estimate by the U.S. government for 1976 showed that over a half-million hectares were disrupted by surface mining. Of this, roughly two thirds was from the mining of nonfuel minerals and one third was from coal. Although some countries have strict regulations on land restoration after strip mining, the more common result is wasteland of the sort that can now be seen in the brown coal mining regions of eastern Germany. Once the mining is completed, the devastated landscape is reminiscent of the surface of the moon.[5]

The first check on the worldwide rush to a throwaway society came during the seventies as oil prices and environmental consciousness climbed. Rising energy costs made recycling more attractive, slowing the trend toward tossing out even more metal, glass, and paper. The second boost came during the eighties as many urban landfill sites filled, forcing municipal governments to ship their garbage to faraway places for disposal. For example, in many U.S. cities, garbage disposal costs during the last decade increased severalfold, making it cost-effective for them to help establish recycling industries.[6]

During the nineties, this trend will be reinforced by the need to reduce carbon emissions, air pollution, acid rain, and toxic waste. In the early stages, countries will move toward comprehensive, systematic recycling of metal, glass, paper, and other materials, beginning with source separation at the consumer level. Many communities in Europe, Japan, and, more recently, the United States have already taken steps in this direction.

Steady advances in technologies are speeding the transition. Electric arc furnaces produce high-quality steel from scrap metal using far less energy than an antiquated open-hearth furnace does. In the United States, a leader in this technology, roughly a third of all steel is already produced from scrap in such furnaces. They can operate wherever there is electricity and a supply of scrap metal, and they can be built on a scale adapted to the volume of locally available scrap. Feeding on worn-out automobiles, household appliances, and industrial equipment, their geographic distribution will reflect that of population. Further, they will provide local jobs and revenue, while eliminating a source of waste.[7]

In the sustainable economy of the future, the principal source of materials for industry will be recycled goods. Most of the raw material for the aluminum mill would come from the local scrap collection center, not from the bauxite mine. Paper and paper products would be produced at recycling mills, with recycled paper moving through a hierarchy of uses, from high-quality bond through newsprint and, eventually, into cardboard boxes. When the recycled fibers are finally no longer reusable, they can be composted or burned as fuel in a cogenerating plant. In a paper products industry that continually uses recycled materials, wood pulp will play a minor role. In mature industrial societies with stable populations, industries will feed largely on what is already within the system, turning to virgin raw materials only to replace any losses in use and recycling.

Although solid waste generation is on the rise in most industrial nations, some countries are now attempting to move beyond the throwaway society. Germany is taking the lead by putting pressure on manufacturers and retailers to assume responsibility for waste from their products and packaging. One response has been that German automobile manufacturers—including BMW, Daimler-Benz, and Volkswagen—are working to make disassembly and reuse of vehicle components much easier, and have set up pilot recycling programs.[8]

In the recycling of household appliances such as refrigerators, Germany is a pioneer in reusing all the materials they contain, including chlorofluorocarbons (CFCs). With a typical refrigerator containing more than a kilogram of CFCs, the family of chemicals that is both depleting the stratospheric ozone layer that protects us from ultraviolet radiation and accounting for roughly one fifth of the rise in greenhouse gases, this is a major advance. The German technology recaptures CFCs both from the compressor and from the foam insulation used in the refrigerator.[9]

Not only is this technology helping protect the future habitability of the planet, it is also yielding economic benefits. As other countries, most immediately Sweden and Switzerland, decide to recycle refrigerators, they are importing the CFC reclamation equipment developed in Germany.[10]

With beverage containers, which account for a substantial share of the garbage flow from a typical household, Denmark has moved to the forefront. In 1977, it banned the use of throwaway containers for soft drinks, and in 1981 it did the same for beer containers. With these bans, Denmark was accused of discriminating against beverages from other countries and charged with protectionism by the other members of the European Community. Fortunately, its argument that environmental protection took precedence over trade policy was sustained in the European Court of Justice. (See also Chapter 10.)[11]

Although early moves away from the throwaway society are concentrating on recycling, sustainability over the long term depends more on eliminating waste flows. One of the most obvious places to reduce the volume of waste generated is in industry, where a restructuring of manufacturing processes can easily slash wastes by a third or more. A trailblazer in this field, the 3M Company halved its hazardous waste flows within a decade of launching a corporation-wide program, boosting its profits in the process and leading other companies to re-examine their manufacturing technologies.[12]

Scientists at AT&T's Bell Laboratories, for example, are redesigning their manufacturing operations to eliminate waste generation. Early successes have led to a set of corporate goals for AT&T's worldwide operations, employing some 275,000 workers. Prominent among these are the phaseout of all CFC use by the end of 1994, a 95-percent reduction in toxic air emissions by the end of 1995, a reduction in waste from manufacturing processes of 25 percent by the end of 1994, a reduction in paper use of 15 percent by 1994, and a 35-percent paper recycling rate by the end of 1994. Conspicuously absent from the list are goals for reducing carbon emissions and toxic wastes. Including these would permit the comprehensive restructuring of industrial processes that holds the key to building an environmentally sustainable global economy.[13]

Another major potential source of waste reduction lies in the simplification of food packaging. In the United States, consumer expenditures on food packaging now routinely approach or even exceed the net income of farmers. In the interest of attracting customers, items are sometimes buried in three or four layers of wrappings. For the final trip from supermarket to home, yet another set of materials is used in the form of paper or plastic bags, also typically discarded after one use. In an environmentally sustainable world, excessive packaging is likely to be eliminated, either by consumer resistance, a packaging tax, or governmental regulations, and throwaway grocery bags will have been replaced by durable, reusable bags of canvas or other material.[14]

Societies may also decide to replace multisized and shaped beverage containers with a set of standardized ones made of durable glass that can be reused many times. These could be used for most if not all beverages, such as fruit juices, beer, milk, and soft drinks. Bottlers will simply clean the container, steam off the old label, and add a new one. Containers returned to the supermarket or other outlet might become part of an urban or regional computerized inventory, which would permit their efficient movement from supermarkets or other collection centers to local dairies, breweries, and soft drink bottling plants as needed.

Such a system would save an enormous amount of energy and materials. Going to refillable glass bottles that are used an average of 10 times can reduce the energy use per container by 90 percent. (See Table 4–1.) The Canadian province of Ontario, where 84 percent of beer is sold in standardized refillable glass bottles, is already moving in this direction. With a stiff deposit, 98 percent of these refillable bottles are returned for reuse. If the goal is to satisfy human needs as fully as possible without disrupting the earth's ecosystem, then the attraction of refillable glass bottles for the marketing of beverages is obvious.[15]

In addition to reusing and recycling metal, glass, and paper, a sustainable society also recycles nutrients. In nature, one organism's waste is another's sustenance; in urban societies, however, human sewage has become a troublesome source of pollutants in rivers, lakes, and coastal waters. The nutrients in human wastes can be reused safely as long as the process includes measures to prevent the spread of disease.

Cities in Japan, South Korea, and China have long demonstrated this kind of nutrient recycling. Human waste is systematically returned there to the land in vegetable-growing greenbelts around cities. Intensively farmed cropland surrounding some urban areas produces vegetables year-round using greenhouses or plastic covering during the winter to extend the growing season. Perhaps the best model is Shanghai: after modestly

TABLE 4-1. *Energy Consumption Per Use for 12-Ounce Beverage Containers*

Container	Energy Use
	(Btus)
Aluminum Can, Used Once	7,050
Steel Can, Used Once	5,950
Recycled Steel Can	3,880
Glass Beer Bottle, Used Once	3,730
Recycled Aluminum Can	2,550
Recycled Glass Beer Bottle	2,530
Refillable Glass Bottle, Used 10 Times	610

SOURCE: See endnote 15.

expanding its urban political boundaries to facilitate
sewage recycling, the city now produces a surplus of
vegetables that are exported to other cities in China.[16]

Some cities will probably find it more efficient to use
treated human sewage to fertilize aquacultural operations. A steady flow of nutrients from human waste into
ponds can supply food for a vigorously growing population of algae that in turn are consumed by fish. In Cal-
cutta, a sewage-fed aquaculture system now provides
20,000 kilograms of fresh fish each day for sale in the
city. In a society with a scarcity of protein, such an approach, modeled after nature's nutrient recycling, can
both eliminate a troublesome waste problem and generate a valuable food resource.[17]

Strong community recycling programs will include
composting of food and yard wastes, which now make
up one fourth of U.S. garbage. People will have the option of composting at home or, if they are unable to do
so, putting such wastes out for curbside pickup. A lost
art in many communities, household composting is
being fostered in Seattle, Washington, by a volunteer
network of "master composters." Composting not only
reduces garbage flows, it provides a rich source of
humus for gardening, lessening the need to buy chemical fertilizers to maintain lawn and garden fertility.[18]

By systematically reducing the flow of waste and reusing or recycling most remaining materials, the basic
needs of the planet's growing number of human residents can be satisfied without destroying our very life-
support systems. Moving in this direction will not only
create a far more livable environment with less air and
water pollution, it will also eliminate the unsightly litter
that blights the landscape in many industrial societies
today.

5

Protecting
the Biological Base

Four biological systems—forests, grasslands, fisheries, and croplands—supply all of our food and much of the raw materials for industry, with the notable exceptions of fossil fuels and minerals. Forests supply lumber, paper, and fuel; grasslands and fisheries supply much of the animal protein in our diets; croplands supply most of the carbohydrates, plus vegetable fibers and oils, and a wide array of other raw materials for industry. The first three systems are discussed in this chapter, leaving croplands to be discussed in more detail in Chapter 6.

Each of these systems is fueled by photosynthesis, the process by which plants use solar energy to combine water and carbon dioxide to form carbohydrates. Indeed, this process for converting solar energy into biochemical energy supports all life on earth, including the

5.4 billion members of our species. Unless we manage these basic biological systems more intelligently than we now are, the earth will never meet the basic needs of 8 billion people.

Photosynthesis is the common currency of biological systems, the yardstick by which their output can be aggregated and changes in their productivity measured. Although the estimated 41 percent of photosynthetic activity that takes place in the oceans supplies us with seafood, it is the 59 percent occurring on land that supports the world economy. And it is the loss of terrestrial photosynthesis as a result of environmental degradation that is undermining many national economies.[1]

Each year, human activities whittle away at our photosynthetic foundation. Large areas are destroyed outright through the paving of land for roads and parking lots, the clearing of forests, and the conversion of farms and woodlands to housing subdivisions and shopping malls. Even greater areas are degraded from air pollution and acid rain, overgrazing, poor farming methods, and destructive logging.

Aside from these assaults, the excessive demands on natural biological systems also reduces their output. Of the basic four, three of them—forests, grasslands, and fisheries—are essentially "natural" ones. Their carrying capacity (the level of demand they can sustain) is a function of their size and regenerative powers and of how they are managed, as well as of less predictable natural factors. Once the carrying capacity is exceeded, the natural system begins to deteriorate. A grassland, for example, will support a set number of cattle or a somewhat larger number of sheep. Where herds grow too large, they will decimate grazing lands; as erosion exacts its toll, these pastures turn into barren wastelands.

With forests, the effect of excessive harvesting is highly visible as deforestation. In scores of countries, people are consuming nature's capital along with the interest it provides. Already a third less than in preagricultural times, the earth's forests are shrinking by more than 17 million hectares per year. Ending the destruction of tropical forests is essential to safeguarding the earth's biological diversity, stabilizing climate, and maintaining a well-functioning hydrological cycle. Achieving a sustainable global economy depends on dramatically slowing deforestation during the nineties and reversing the trend soon thereafter.[2]

What would forests look like, and how would they be used in a sustainable world? Efforts to protect unique parcels of forest will probably have led to a widely dispersed network of preserves. In recent years, biologists have identified 15 "hotspots"—tropical forests in which biological diversity is especially at risk—that account for about 12 percent of all tropical rain forest remaining but that contain a third to half of all the world's plant species. Protecting these areas is key to conserving the planet's biological wealth, and may be the only way of slowing the unprecedented pace of species extinctions now under way.[3]

Although some areas will require strict preservation with minimal human use, a large portion of tropical forests still standing over the long term can be exploited in a variety of ways by people living in and around them. Hundreds of "extractive reserves" can exist, areas in which local people harvest rubber, resins, nuts, fruits, medicinal substances, and other nontimber forest products for domestic use or export. Studies suggest that the long-term economic benefits of managing rain forests this way are greater than those derived from burning off an equivalent area and planting it in crops or pasture. Although the latter two uses yield greater monetary returns in the initial few years after clearing, before long income drops to zero when the land's productivity is gone. If the environmental benefits could be quantified and added in, the balance would tip even more clearly in favor of leaving the forest intact.[4]

By definition, a sustainable society does not overcut or degrade its forests for lumber or other wood products. Logging operations in both tropical and temperate countries today often damage or destroy large areas. A 1989 study for the International Tropical Timber Organization came to the astonishing conclusion that less than 0.1 percent of tropical logging was being done on a sustained-yield basis. And for each 10-hectare clear-cut of virgin forest in the U.S. Pacific Northwest, an additional 14 hectares are degraded from exposure to wind, exotic species, and local climatic changes.[5]

Glimpses of a "new forestry" have appeared in recent years, an approach that views forests as complex ecosystems providing a multitude of benefits, rather than simply as suppliers of lumber and fiber. Logging is carried out in a manner that minimizes destruction and enables the forests' rapid recovery. Promising efforts in the Siskiyou National Forest in Oregon and the Palcazu Valley in Peru are providing valuable insights into how human needs for wood can be met while protecting natural forests' integrity.[6]

Protecting forests also requires much greater efficiency in our use of wood. In the United States, the world's largest wood consumer, simply raising the efficiency of forest product manufacturing to levels approached in Japan would save enough wood to leave standing one out of four trees now cut nationwide. Together, available methods of reducing waste, increasing efficiency, and boosting recycling of paper and other wood products could cut U.S. wood consumption by half.[7]

Along with better natural forest management and more efficient wood use, planting vast additional areas in trees is essential. Meeting fuelwood needs and stabilizing soil and water resources in developing countries will require planting trees on some 130 million hectares—an area slightly larger than Ethiopia—over the next decade or so. Large areas of partially desertified land, degraded watersheds, railroad and highway borders, and open countryside would need to be reforested for this target to be met. Because trees absorb carbon from the atmosphere as they grow, planting more of them can also help slow the pace of global warming. This gives industrial countries good reason to step up tree planting within their own borders, as well as to aid developing countries in doing so.[8]

Many of these plantings could be on private farms as part of agroforestry systems. (See Chapter 6 for further discussion of agroforestry.) But plantations may also have an expanded role. Cities and villages can turn to managed woodlands on their outskirts to contribute fuel for heating, cooking, and electricity. Wood from these plantations could substitute for some portion of coal and oil use, and, if harvested on a sustained-yield basis, would make no net contribution of carbon dioxide to the atmosphere.

The second biological system, grasslands, would also be managed differently in a sustainable world. Once the plow has run its course, most of the unforested land that remains is good for grazing only. Almost without exception, agricultural land too dry or too steeply sloping to sustain cultivation is used to support livestock. Roughly double the area in crops, the 24 percent of the earth's land surface (over 3 billion hectares) devoted to this purpose supports nearly 3 billion domesticated ruminants, about half of them cattle and most of the rest, goats and sheep.[9]

These ruminant herds and flocks play an indispensable role in the world economy. Unlike pigs, chickens, and people, whose diets consist primarily of cereals and other concentrated food, ruminants are equipped to digest roughage and to convert it into forms people can use. The role of ruminants depends on their unique capacity to digest cellulose, the world's most abundant organic compound. Capable of subsisting solely on grasses or even foliage from shrubs and trees, livestock provide food in the form of meat, milk, cheese, and butter. They also supply other essential commodities: fuel, fertilizer, and industrial raw materials, such as leather, wool, and tallow. The world's leather goods and footwear industry depend heavily on cattle hides, and wool remains one of the world's premium textile fibers. In addition, an estimated one third of the world's cropland is tilled by draft animals that live almost entirely on forage.[10]

Although the data for grassland degradation are even more sketchy than those for forest clearing, the trends appear equally disturbing. Excessively large herds have degraded an estimated 73 percent of the world's rangeland. This problem is highly visible throughout Africa, where livestock numbers have expanded from nearly 272 million in 1950 to some 560 million in 1988, an increase that closely parallels the continent's growth in human population from 283 million to 610 million.[11]

The key to putting livestock production on a sustainable footing is to reduce herds to a number that grass-lands can sustain. Difficult though this may be, it is the only alternative to continuing degradation of grasslands and the eventual decline in livestock numbers from widespread starvation of the sort now particularly evident during drought years in Africa and the Indian subcontinent.

In the effort to establish a sustainable balance, more farmers could integrate livestock into their diverse farming systems, using for fodder the protein-rich leaves from leguminous trees in their agroforestry systems or the cover crop in their rotational cropping patterns. In densely populated countries such as India, many could stall-feed their herds, rather than allowing them to range freely. In a hilly region of the north Indian state of Haryana, the experimental closure of a small watershed to cattle led to a fourfold rise in the annual yield of fodder grasses within seven years. Where feasible, this may hold the key to regenerating grasslands and restoring fodder supplies for livestock.[12]

One practice that can help sustain rangeland productivity is rotational grazing, which is widely used in some regions. Rather than ranging freely over a given area, cattle are confined for a time to part of it while the remainder rejuvenates. Although it typically depends on additional fencing, the investment is often worthwhile since it both enhances productivity in the short run and preserves it over the long term. Another procedure that boosts grassland productivity is the grazing of more than one species of ruminants, large and small, on the same land—much as occurs in nature. For example, cattle, which typically prefer grass, are often combined with goats, which like to browse on shrubs. A common practice in parts of Africa, this can protect vegetation from excessive pressure by reducing the number of cattle or goats while boosting the sustainable yield of livestock products.

The third natural biological system, fisheries, occupies an important niche in the global ecosystem and the human diet. The annual harvest from oceanic and freshwater fisheries—in excess of 90 million tons per year in the late eighties—exceeds world beef production by a substantial margin. Yielding an average of 18.5 kilograms per capita live weight, fisheries supply almost a quarter of all animal protein consumed by humans. More important, fish are the primary source of animal protein in many low-income countries.[13]

Throughout most of human history, far more fish swam in the oceans than we could ever hope to catch. Indeed, the fish in the sea seemed as plentiful as those in the New Testament parable. But as human numbers moved from 3 billion to 4 billion and then beyond 5 billion, the global appetite for table-grade fish exceeded the regenerative capacity of more and more fisheries. Overfishing led to shrinking stocks, declining catches, and rising seafood prices. The past few decades have been marked by the collapse of one fishery after another—the Northeast Atlantic herring, the Atlantic cod, and the Northwest Pacific salmon, to cite a few. Although initially confined to the North Atlantic, collapses have now occurred in all the world's oceans.[14]

Freshwater fisheries are threatened not only by overfishing, but by acid rain as well. Thousands of freshwater lakes in the northern hemisphere, particularly in Scandinavia, are now entirely devoid of fish. The destruction of estuaries by industrial pollution and agricultural runoff is also taking a toll. That part of the aquatic environment where "the flow of the river meets the flood of the tide," estuaries are a major spawning area and breeding place for migratory fish; they are also the common habitat of shellfish.[15]

Diverting water from streams that feed inland water bodies presents another problem. The Soviet Union's Aral Sea yielded more than 40 million kilograms of fish annually as recently as 1960. Since then, the diversion for irrigation of water from the two rivers that feed that sea has led to its shrinkage. As it lost 40 percent of its area and 65 percent of its volume, the salt concentration climbed to the point where few fish could survive. The fishing industry has long since collapsed.[16]

Maintaining fisheries productivity depends on policy adjustments in the larger economy as well as in the industry itself. Within the fisheries sector, limiting the catch to the sustainable yield holds the key to maintaining future productivity. In areas where freshwater fisheries are threatened by acid rain, the solution is to reduce the use of fossil fuels or install scrubbers on power plant smokestacks and catalytic converters on automobile exhausts. For the Soviet Union's Aral Sea, it is more a matter of restoring the freshwater inflow that sustains the sea, a step that depends on using irrigation water more efficiently.

Yet another possibility for protecting oceanic fisheries is for our consumption to move down the food chain, eating more of the less desirable species. This, in fact, has been happening over the last few decades as greater quantities of Alaska pollock, Atlantic mackerel, and shark have made their way onto dinner tables.[17]

An expansion of fish farming can also alleviate the economic pressure on natural fisheries. Recent years have seen enormous growth in this area, ranging from catfish farming in the southern United States to salmon ranching in Norway and Scotland. Asia, the traditional leader in fish farming, continues to expand its aquacultural output. Even though fish farming helps reduce the pressure on fisheries, it is not a panacea; it requires not only land but also water, itself an increasingly scarce resource.[18]

While in most cases the technical means exist to restore and stabilize the planet's biological resource base, there are many economic and social impediments. Much of the land degradation now occurring, for example, stems from the heavily skewed distribution that, along with population growth, pushes more people into ever more marginal environments. Good stewardship requires that people have plots large enough to sustain their families without abusing the land, access to the technological means of using their land productively, and the right to pass it on to their children.[19]

This inevitably will require large landholdings in densely populated agrarian societies to be broken up and redistributed to the poor who lack viable livelihoods. Similarly, much government-owned common land, including forests and pastures, likely will revert to communities and villages that have a stake in optimizing the productivity of these lands and managing them sustainably. Zimbabwe is about the only country that in recent years has started to undertake meaningful land reform; the political will has so far been lacking in most nations where it is needed.[20]

No matter what technologies and engineering feats come along in the future, human survival depends on a healthy biological base. Protecting the planet's biological resources before irreversible thresholds are breached presents a monumental challenge. Unlikely as it may seem, success hinges as much on energy policies and family planning programs as it does on the management skills of fishers, ranchers, and foresters.

6

Grain
for Eight Billion

Adequately feeding 8 billion people may be the single most difficult task in building a sustainable world. We are exploring the outer reaches of the solar system, reaping the benefits of the computer revolution, and working wonders in medicine, but as the nineties progress, the ranks of the hungry are expanding. The growth in world output of grain, the staff of life, has slowed dramatically in recent years.

Although fisheries and grasslands supply much of the animal protein in our diet, it is croplands—and specifically, the grains grown on them—that supply the bulk of our food. Grains consumed directly account for half of human food energy and indirectly, in the form of meat, milk, eggs, butter, and cheese, a large share of the remainder. With the demands on oceanic fisheries and grasslands now commonly exceeding sustainable yields, the world is heavily dependent on croplands to satisfy future food needs. Eliminating hunger among an estimated 900 million people and providing for nearly 3 billion more will require pushing the current world grain harvest of 1.7 billion tons to some 2.7 billion—a feat that will tax the ingenuity of the world's farmers.[1]

Between 1950 and 1984, farmers raised global grain output 2.6-fold, an increase that dwarfed the efforts of all previous generations combined. During this 34 years, the annual growth of 3 percent per year raised per capita grain consumption one third, banishing hunger from much of the world. Unfortunately, from 1984 to 1990 food output growth dropped to 1 percent per year, scarcely half that of population. This disturbing trend signals a new era, one in which an acceptable balance between food and people cannot be achieved with a business-as-usual approach.[2]

As the nineties unfold, increasing difficulties in expanding cropland area and irrigation water supplies are constraining the growth of world food output. In addition, the effects of environmental degradation, such as soil erosion and air pollution, are beginning to show up at harvest time.

Growth in the world's cultivated area, which slowed rather abruptly at mid-century, came to a halt around 1980. Each year millions of hectares of cropland are lost either because the land is so severely eroded it is not worth plowing anymore or because it is converted to nonfarm uses, used to build homes and factories on, or paved over for highways and parking lots.[3]

Some countries, such as Brazil, may be able to add new cropland in the years ahead. China, on the other hand, has lost an average of 500,000 hectares of cropland annually to nonfarm uses over the last three decades. Although the United States and a few other industrial countries can return to production the cropland idled under commodity programs, on balance gains and losses in the decades ahead are likely to largely offset each other, as they did during the eighties. As a result, the steady shrinkage in cropland area per person under way since mid-century will continue as long as population grows.[4]

With little prospect of expanding the cultivated area, satisfying future food needs thus depends on raising the productivity of existing cropland. In densely populated developing countries, where labor is abundant relative to land, this effort can center on multiple cropping, intercropping, and other practices that raise land use intensity. Multiple cropping simply means growing more than one crop per year on the same area of land. China, Japan, South Korea, and Taiwan have all achieved an annual average of 1.1 to 1.5 crops per hectare.[5]

Intercropping—growing two or more crops at the same time—can also boost output. Often legumes and cereal crops are combined; the legumes fix nitrogen in the soil for nitrogen-hungry cereals. In another approach, crops overlap. As one crop is nearing maturity, another is planted between its rows. When the first crop is harvested, the other is already well-established and growing rapidly. In northern China, for example, farmers seed corn in their fields of winter wheat shortly before harvesting it in early summer.[6]

A variation on this is transplanting, a practice widely used by Asian rice growers. Instead of directly seeding a crop, such as rice, in a field, farmers plant the seeds in a seedbed and then transplant the young seedlings directly into the field. In parts of Asia this shortens the cropping period enough to permit double-cropping of rice or of rice and wheat.

As noted, the best models for raising land productivity are in East Asia. In countries where agricultural land-ownership is concentrated in a few hands, more intensive use depends on land reform. In Latin America, where wealthy landowners often graze cattle on fertile land suited to cropping, such reforms would shift land use from cattle grazing to food production. Adequately feeding 8 billion people in an environmentally sustainable manner depends on the intensive use of all the planet's productive cropland.[7]

Although the prospect for expanding world irrigated area is slightly more promising than that for the cultivated area, it is diminishing. After growing slowly during this century's first half, the irrigated area climbed rapidly from 94 million hectares in 1950 to 211 million in 1980. As investment in both large water projects and farmer-owned wells and pumps soared, irrigation grew far faster than population, expanding the irrigated area per person by a record 27 percent during this three-decade span.[8]

By 1980, however, most of the economically attractive sites for large dams and reservoirs had been developed; the expansion in world irrigated area slowed dramatically, falling behind population growth. Between 1978 and 1988, the irrigated area per person shrank by 6 percent. (See Figure 6–1.) Although the cropland area per person has been decreasing steadily since mid-century, this irrigation trend is new, making the eighties the first decade in which both have declined. This, too, may help explain the recent slowdown in food output growth.[9]

Just as satisfying future food needs depends on using

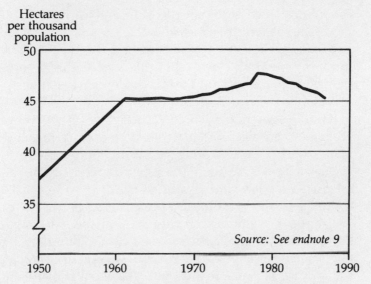

FIGURE 6-1. *World Net Irrigated Area Per Capita, 1950-87*

land more intensively, so too it depends on using water more efficiently. With the amount of fresh water produced by the hydrological cycle essentially fixed by nature, raising efficiency is the key to producing more food where water is already scarce. Fortunately, there are vast opportunities for increasing water efficiency. From California's irrigated valleys to the Soviet Union's Aral Sea basin, the delivery of water from large public irrigation projects to farmers either free or for a low cost leads to its wasteful use.

A shift to market pricing of water could encourage farmers to adopt more water-efficient technologies and to plant more water-efficient crops. For example, when farmers pay the full cost of water, they are apt to grow more wheat and less rice, simply because a ton of wheat can be produced with half the water. Opportunities for increasing water efficiency abound, though some such as drip irrigation, are capital-intensive. Israel, a pioneer in raising water efficiency, has developed a highly productive irrigated agriculture in a desert environment despite severe water constraints.[10]

Rainfed agriculture, which accounts for 83 percent of cropland, can also benefit from better water management. When water scarcity leads to food scarcity in semiarid regions, various water harvesting methods can be used to raise land productivity. One widely used technique involves building a terrace or ridge of rocks or soil across the slope, sometimes planting food or forage-bearing trees on the terrace to collect rainfall runoff. As the trapped water is absorbed into the soil, enough can accumulate to produce a crop. If the catchment is kept small, a few hectares or less, farmers can do this entirely with local resources.[11]

At a slightly more sophisticated level, farmers can build small earthen dams to collect rainfall for irrigation. As water scarcity increasingly constrains food output growth, these small-scale storage structures at the individual farm or village level are likely to become more popular as a means of gaining control over local water resources.

Since mid-century, the expanding use of chemical fertilizers has been the engine behind the growth in world food output, climbing from a meager 14 million tons in 1950 to 144 million tons in 1990. As new land for cropping became scarce, farmers had little choice but to turn to fertilizers to raise land productivity as they tried to satisfy growing world food needs. As urbanization removed people from the land and as mixed grain/livestock farming was replaced with specialized grain and livestock enterprises, the traditional recycling of nutrients was disrupted, making farmers more dependent on chemical fertilizer to replace the nutrients lost in the crops they sold.[12]

The contribution of two other yield-raising inputs— irrigation and high-yielding varieties—derives heavily from their ability to boost the effectiveness of fertilizer. As the transition from fossil fuels to solar energy progresses, the production of fertilizers, especially energy-intensive nitrogen ones, will rely increasingly on renewable energy.

In some countries, including the United States, fertilizer use has levelled off, changing little since 1980. In others, such as Argentina, India, and Nigeria, the potential of boosting food output by using more fertilizer remains promising. Exploiting this can provide some of the additional food needed while the world tries to complete the shift to smaller families.[13]

While cropland per person shrunk by 40 percent from 1950 through the mid-eighties, fertilizer use per person multiplied nearly five times—rising from 5.5 kilograms to 26. Since then, however, this substitution of fertilizer for land has slowed, raising questions about the ability of farmers to restore a rapid rise of food output and underlining the urgency of slowing population growth. (See Figure 6–2.)[14]

Feeding more people also depends on more nutrient recycling. As pressures on the land intensify, other developing regions are likely to follow the East Asian lead and begin to assiduously collect all human and livestock waste and other organic materials to use for fertilizer. In addition to supplying valuable nutrients, the organic matter improves soil structure and boosts land productivity.

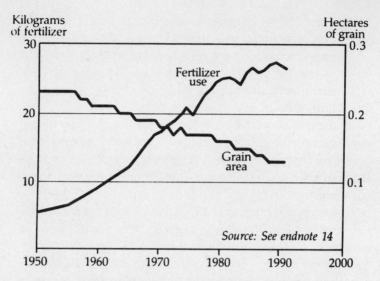

FIGURE 6-2. *World Fertilizer Use Per Person and Grain Area Per Person, 1950-91*

As farmers face the prospect of feeding nearly 3 billion additional people, they must cope with the adverse effects of environmental degradation—some of their own making, and some from outside agriculture. Reports of land degradation have come from every corner of the planet. In July 1989, Australian Prime Minister Robert Hawke said that "none of Australia's environmental problems is more serious than the soil degradation . . .over nearly two thirds of our continent's arable land." Pravda reports that the Soviet Union is suffering from a catastrophic decline in soil fertility.[15]

The effect of topsoil losses on U.S. land productivity has been well established, showing that a worldwide effort to conserve soil is an indispensable component of a hunger elimination strategy. Results from 14 studies on corn, done mostly in the Corn Belt states, showed that a loss of one inch of topsoil reduced yields by an average of 6 percent. Twelve studies on wheat showed a similar loss.[16]

As farmers try to preserve and raise land productivity, rural landscapes are likely to exhibit greater diversity than they do now. Farmers can exploit variations in soils, climate, and water availability by turning to different patterns of production so as to maximize sustainable output. For instance, many are likely to adopt numerous forms of agroforestry—the combined production of crops and trees. Agroforestry can provide high yields of food, biomass for energy, and fodder for livestock, while also adding nutrients to the soil and controlling water runoff.[17]

Although agroforestry is an age-old practice, it has acquired new stature over the last decade as a sustainable form of land use able to help meet people's basic needs. In Haiti, for example, the most poverty-stricken and degraded country in the western hemisphere, a system known as alley cropping is showing much potential. Farmers plant hedgerows of nitrogen-fixing trees along the contours of gently sloping land, seeding crops between them. A natural terrace forms behind each hedgerow, controlling soil erosion and thus also conserving nutrients and moisture. The trees' leaves can be used as a green mulch or as animal fodder, while well-timed pruning offers a source of much-needed fuelwood. Though no detailed analyses of the decade-old project have been done yet, crop yields appear to have increased along with soil and water conservation.[18]

One of the most celebrated agroforestry efforts in a dry region is that of Niger's Majjia Valley. There, rows of trees have been planted on farmland as a break on the intense winds that whip away topsoil and damage young plants. Between 1975 and 1988, some 463 kilometers of neem trees were planted, protecting more than 4,600 hectares of cropland. Average windspeeds in the protected areas dropped about 40 percent. Despite the cropland taken up by the windbreaks, 90 percent of the villagers asked about the project said they were benefiting from it. The newly planted trees also provided valuable wood for poles and firewood, again illustrating agroforestry's potential to satisfy several basic needs simultaneously.[19]

One simple solution in the fight against land degradation is the planting of hearty grasses along the contours of sloping farmlands. Vetiver grass, native to India and known there as *khus*, has proved a good candidate for many areas, effectively controlling erosion for less than 10 percent of the cost of building earthen or rock walls. When closely spaced along the contours of a hillside, vetiver grass forms a vegetative barrier that slows runoff, giving rainfall a chance to spread out and seep into a field. It also traps sediment behind it, gradually forming a natural terrace. From the soil and moisture conserved this way, yields have often increased by half.[20]

In a remote corner of China's Loess Plateau, among the most degraded areas on earth, a partnership of villagers, scientists, political leaders, and international development agencies has dramatically improved both the land and rural people's livelihoods. In the village of Quanjiagou, for instance, trees and fodder shrubs were planted on the hillsides, soil-trapping earthen dams were constructed across the mouths of gullies, and impressive tiers of terraces were formed up the fertile slopes—all to control soil erosion. Aided by new crop varieties suited to this locale, harvests increased 17 percent between 1979 and 1986, even though the area planted in crops was reduced by half. With the added value from cash-crop tree products and animal husbandry, the village's per capita income more than doubled.[21]

The only major food producer with a successful nationwide program to protect its soils is the United States, which reduced its erosion losses by more than one third between 1985 and 1990, and is expected to reduce it by another one third by 1995. (See Table 6–1.) Gains during the first five years came almost entirely from converting 14 million hectares of highly erodible cropland, roughly one tenth of the total cropland area, to grass or trees. Eliminating the remaining erosion depends on adjusting cropping patterns and shifting to minimum tillage or no-till agricultural practices. Accounting for one sixth of world grain output, the United States provides a timely example that other countries can look to. Obviously each country will have to fashion its own soil conservation strategy, but the U.S. success provides a starting point.[22]

TABLE 6-1. *United States: Progress in Reducing Soil Erosion from Croplands, 1986–90, With Projections to 1995*

Soil Loss	Million Tons
Excessive soil loss in 1985	1,600
Reduction, 1986–90	−600
Projected reduction, 1991–95	−450
Remaining excessive soil erosion	550

SOURCE: See endnote 22.

Some progress is also being made on reversing the generation-long trend of rising pesticide use—a practice being reexamined because of the threat to human health, the endangerment of other species, and rising pest resistance. Many U.S. farmers are turning to integrated pest management, a technique that relies on crop rotations, the use of natural enemies of pests, and pest-resistant crop varieties as well as the selective use of chemicals. Some countries have gone even further than this: Indonesia, for example, banned the use of 57 pesticides on rice in late 1986.[23]

Satisfying future food needs also depends on reversing the trends of environmental degradation originating outside agriculture that are now showing up at harvest time, such as deforestation, air pollution, and, quite possibly, global warming. Reversing deforestation can help reduce the frequency of crop-damaging floods. Adopting the agroforestry practices discussed earlier can also help alleviate the firewood scarcity that is forcing villagers to use cow dung and crop residues for cooking fuel.

Phasing out fossil fuels is the key to stabilizing climate and minimizing disruption in agriculture. The drought- and heat-damaged U.S. grain harvest in 1988, which fell below domestic consumption for the first time in history, gives us a glimpse of how hotter summers may affect agriculture over the longer term. Moving away from fossil fuels will also help reduce the air pollution that, according to official estimates, has lowered the U.S. harvest by at least 5 percent, and possibly as much as 10 percent.[24]

One of the unanswered questions hanging over the world's food future is whether any dramatic technological advance can lead to a quantum jump in world grain output over the next few decades comparable to that coming from fertilizer over the past generation. Unfortunately, no such development is in prospect. Advances in biotechnology are helping to develop pest-resistant crop strains, earlier maturing crops, and even salt-tolerant food and forage crops. But while all of these are helpful, they will not add the vast amounts of food needed to feed nearly 3 billion more people. In the absence of any technological panaceas, future gains are likely to come largely from using land more intensively and diversely, water more efficiently, and more fertilizer where it is profitable to do so.

Efforts to eliminate hunger could be strengthened by a reduction in consumption of livestock products among the billion or so wealthiest people in the world. Rapidly accumulating medical evidence indicates that even moderate consumption of livestock products can reduce life expectancy. As public awareness of this spreads, it could lead the world's affluent to eat further down on the food chain, thus reducing the share of grain consumed by livestock and freeing up more for direct human consumption.

Producing enough grain for 8 billion people depends partly on the efforts of farmers and partly on the success of governments and international development agencies in dealing with the broader environmental threats. Indeed, efforts to stabilize population and climate may have a far greater effect on attempts to achieve a satisfactory balance between food and people than anything agricultural policymakers themselves can do.

In modern, postindustrial societies, where most people do not remain on the land and are thus largely isolated from the economy's agricultural foundations, there is a tendency to take the land's capacity to satisfy

our needs for granted. But as Harvard ecological an-
thropologist Timothy Weiskel quite rightly notes,
"There is no such thing as a 'post-agricultural' society."
Feeding 8 billion people in an environmentally sustainable manner depends on investing far more time and capital in agriculture than we are now doing—in short, giving it the priority it deserves.[25]

7

A Stable
World Population

People living in industrial countries, with their high levels of affluence, are causing a disproportionately large share of the damage being done to the earth's natural systems. The average American today, for example, consumes 36 times as much commercial energy as the average Indian, and thus contributes far more to global warming, acid rain, and air pollution. The challenge in these wealthier societies, where populations are growing slowly or not at all, is to reduce resource consumption along the lines laid out in previous chapters on energy, materials, and food.[1]

In developing countries, however, the sheer number of people being added each year is a growing threat to the environment and its ability to sustain the population. Well-being in the Third World is closely tied to the quality and abundance of the resources people depend on to meet their daily needs—productive soils, fodder for their animals, wood for heating and cooking, and clean water. In many parts of the developing world, human numbers are beginning to overwhelm local resources, leading to a deteriorating resource base and falling living standards.

Stabilizing world population at a level where basic needs can be satisfied will be extraordinarily difficult. The most recent World Bank projections show the 1991 world population of 5.4 billion growing to at least 12 billion late in the next century. But these numbers ignore the deteriorating condition of local environmental support systems. A world population of 12 billion is unlikely to materialize for the simple reason that natural systems in many countries are already collapsing under existing population and consumption pressures.[2]

If the world remains on the 12-billion-plus trajectory for much longer, population growth will be checked in more and more countries by famine and disease as living standards fall below survival level. Recurrent famine in parts of Africa already takes a heavy toll in human life. The growth of Third World urban populations is spiraling uncontrollably upward, outstripping sanitation services, safe water supplies, and health care facilities. Epidemics, such as the cholera outbreak that began in early 1991 in Peru, could also check future population growth. The World Bank reports that during the eighties, incomes fell in some 40 countries, containing 750 million people. If rapid population growth continues, the number of people trapped in this downward spiral could expand dramatically during the nineties.[3]

We believe human numbers can go no higher than about 8 billion—half again as large as today's population—if the world is to avoid massive deaths from starvation and disease. Considering that one third of all people in the world today are under 15 years of age, and thus have yet to enter their reproductive years, holding world population at this number will take nothing less than a revolution in social values and reproductive behavior. This, in turn, depends on fundamental reforms in many developing countries in education, health care, and the status of women, along with a massive global reordering of priorities.[4]

Population stabilization is obviously easiest in countries where birth rates have been falling for several generations. Thirteen countries have already reached this point, establishing an equilibrium between births and deaths. All are in Europe, and they include three of the continent's most populous countries—Germany, Italy, and the United Kingdom. The others are Austria, Belgium, Bulgaria, Czechoslovakia, Denmark, Greece, Hungary, Luxembourg, Portugal, and Spain. The members of this group have certain things in common: a high standard of living, abundant economic opportunities for women, and readily available family planning services. Altogether, the group contains some 312 million people, roughly 6 percent of the world's population.[5]

Another group of industrial countries, including the largest ones, is moving in the same direction. Now expanding slowly, their rates of natural increase range from 0.3 percent per year in Japan to 0.8 percent in the United States and the Soviet Union. Other European countries, including France and several in Eastern Europe, are also approaching population stability. If these trends continue, a large group of countries, containing some 12 percent of the world's people, will achieve a balance between births and deaths by the end of this decade or shortly thereafter.[6]

In its annual assessment *State of World Population 1991*, the United Nations Population Fund reports that birth rates are now declining in all regions of the Third World. Between 1960–65 and 1985–90, the total fertility rate—the average number of children per woman of childbearing age—for all developing countries fell from an average of 6.1 children per woman to 3.9. This overall average, however, disguised wide variations among regions—a drop from 6.1 to 2.7 in East Asia versus a drop from 6.6 to 6.2 in Africa. Yet fertility is not falling as fast as had earlier been assumed, forcing demographers to revise upward their projections of world population growth.[7]

Notwithstanding falling Third World birth rates, the variation in family size among countries is wider today than at any time in human history. The total fertility rate varies from less than two children in many European countries and Japan to over seven in several countries in Africa and Asia, including Afghanistan, Tanzania, Uganda, and Zambia.[8]

A quick survey of the more populous countries in each region gives a sense of how demographically disparate the world has become. (See Table 7–1.) In the first group, those with fertility near or below the replacement level of two children per couple, some have already reached stability. South Korea, whose fertility level of 1.6 is well below that of the United States, is moving steadily toward population stability. Others, such as China and Thailand, are only a half step away from replacement-level fertility. If they can hold the course they have set for themselves, reducing the average number of children per woman from 2.3 to 2 or less, their popula-

TABLE 7-1. *Total Fertility Rate,
Selected Countries, 1991*

Country	Number of Children[1]
Near or Below Replacement-Level Fertility	
Italy	1.3
Germany	1.5
Japan	1.5
South Korea	1.6
France	1.8
United Kingdom	1.8
United States	2.1
Thailand	2.2
China	2.3
Moderate Fertility Rates	
Sri Lanka	2.5
Colombia	2.9
Indonesia	3.0
Brazil	3.3
Mexico	3.8
India	3.9
High Fertility Rates	
Egypt	4.5
Bangladesh	4.9
Iran	6.2
Nigeria	6.2
Sudan	6.4
Pakistan	6.6
Ethiopia	6.8
Tanzania	7.1

[1]The total fertility rate is the average number of children a woman will have assuming that current age-specific birth rates remain constant throughout her childbearing years.

SOURCE: See endnote 9.

tions will stabilize as the number of young people entering the reproductive years begins to dwindle.[9]

In the moderate-fertility group, Sri Lanka and Colombia are well positioned to bring population growth to a halt. Although average family size in both Mexico and India has been reduced substantially over the past two decades, this goal will be far more difficult for them. Mexico's 1991 population of 86 million is projected by World Bank demographers to approach 200 million before stabilizing. India's population of 859 million is projected to reach nearly 1.9 billion, eclipsing China as the world's most populous country, before it stops growing.[10]

For countries in the high-fertility group, the economic and environmental future is scary to say the least. In Egypt, already dependent on imports for over half its grain, population is projected to nearly triple, putting enormous pressures on its limited land and water resources. The World Bank shows Nigeria's population approaching 600 million, nearly as many as in all of Africa today, before it stops growing late in the next century. And in Ethiopia, where the average family has seven children, numbers are projected to multiply nearly eight times by the end of the twenty-first century. If countries in this latter group continue on such trajectories, environmental collapse is inevitable.[11]

Unless the relationships between rapidly multiplying populations and their life-support systems can be stabilized, development policies—however imaginative—are bound to fail. Against this backdrop, the time has come for world leaders, such as the Secretary General of the United Nations and the President of the World Bank, to speak out on the population issue, making clear the choices that societies now face. For example, halting world population growth at around 8 billion by 2030 or so means moving to replacement-level fertility almost everywhere during this decade. In effect, it means couples stopping at two surviving children—and it means encouraging governments to create the conditions to make this possible.

Difficult though this may be, it is not impossible. Following the loss of its wartime empire in the forties, Japan was forced to adjust quickly to living on the resources within its own national borders. The liberalization of abortion in 1948 was followed by the launching of an official family planning program. As industrialization and urbanization progressed, the advantages of large families diminished. Between 1949 and 1956, Japan's population growth rate dropped from just under 2.2 percent to scarcely 1 percent, a drop described in a U.N. report as "unprecedented in the annals of world demography." Remarkably, Japan made this demographic advance before the advent of modern contraceptives such as the pill and the intrauterine device.[12]

Two decades later, the Chinese government concluded that diminishing per capita resources would undermine its economic progress if continued. In particular, it was concerned with the shrinkage in grainland per person, which had already fallen to 0.12 hectares, one of the smallest in the world. This led to a decision to lower its birth rate quickly. Between 1970 and 1976, China's population growth rate dropped from 2.6 percent per year to 1.3 percent. Like Japan, it cut its growth in half in a matter of years.[13]

At about the same time, Thailand, with a much higher living standard, launched programs to slow its population growth. In contrast to China, it still had 0.21 hectares of grainland per person, enough to produce a large exportable surplus of rice. Accordingly it could afford a more gradual path to population stability. With a charismatic leader, Mechai Viravaidya, forging the way with innovative approaches to both population education and the design of village-level family planning programs, Thailand's average family size started to shrink. Over the last two decades, it has gradually lowered its birth rate until, by 1991, it too was on the verge of achieving replacement-level fertility.[14]

Because Chinese leaders waited too long to face the population issue, people there were forced to choose between lower living standards for their children and an abrupt shift to a one-child family. Unfortunately, many other countries have also delayed in confronting the population threat. Lacking the leadership and the social cohesion to lower their population growth rates quickly, their numbers are being periodically checked by famine. Ethiopia, which has lost much of its topsoil and where farmers now have trouble producing enough food even in years when rainfall is good, tragically exemplifies this alternative.

Given the experiences of Japan, China, and Thailand, a global effort to cut world population growth in half by lowering the number of births during this decade is not out of the question. If the world growth rate is cut to 1 percent by the end of the century, the stage would be set for bringing population growth to a halt at roughly 8 billion by 2030.

Achieving this is not merely a matter of providing basic family planning services. Shifting quickly to smaller families depends on social reforms, such as giving women civil rights and economic opportunities equal to those of men, and on economic commitments that rest on at least partly demilitarizing national economies. Developing countries that have made the shift to small families typically have an active national population education program and widely available family planning services that offer a variety of contraceptive options. In addition, improving economic and social conditions and incentives for small families invariably hastens the fall in fertility.[15]

Making family planning services more accessible to both women and men would dramatically reduce fertility. In Africa, having acceptable contraceptives available to all women who now want them would reduce births by at least one fourth. Some 300 million married couples of reproductive age worldwide have expressed the desire to space or limit births but do not have access to contraceptive methods that fully meet their needs. The U.N. Population Fund estimates that fulfilling this unmet demand for family planning would cost about $9 billion per year, more than double current expenditures—but one fifth the direct U.S. outlay for the 1991 Persian Gulf War.[16]

Expenditures on family planning are even more cost-effective when the resulting health benefits are taken into account. The potential for improvements in women's reproductive health from increased access to family planning is vast. Each year, for example, more than 1 million women die from reproduction-related causes—complications of pregnancy, childbirth, unsafe abortion, and diseases of the reproductive tract. At least 100 million others suffer disabling illness. Helping women to avoid unwanted pregnancy and prevent the transmission of disease through improvements in the supply and availability of contraceptive methods could cut this toll in half. Successful family planning programs yield not only smaller families, but also healthier mothers and children.[17]

Indications are, however, that conventional family

planning programs are ignoring the needs of a large and growing pool of potential clients. The number of unintended pregnancies among unmarried teenagers—leading to unsafe abortions and unwanted births—is on the increase throughout the world. Broadening the concept of unmet need to include this and other currently unrecognized groups would further reduce birth rates and the number of abortions.[18]

As noted, fertility declines most rapidly when family planning services are introduced into a society already enjoying broad-based economic and social gains. The social indicator that is most closely associated with fertility decline is rising literacy among women. Simply put, the more schooling women have, and therefore the more opportunities they have, the fewer children they choose to bear. There are occasional exceptions, but this general relationship holds over a wide spectrum of cultures.[19]

Unfortunately, illiteracy is still far more widespread among women than men. Only 15 percent of all women in Africa are literate, as opposed to 33 percent of the men. Not surprisingly, total fertility rates are highest in African countries. And in many countries, such as Bangladesh, Senegal, and Uganda, barely half the girls of primary school age are now attending classes. Almost all governments have adopted universal primary education as a goal, but few have taken the steps necessary to make education a real possibility for a large share of females.[20]

A number of social and cultural traditions continue to limit public support for educating young girls. One is the need for their labor. Throughout the Third World, girls are expected to assume a work burden that keeps them busy for several hours a day, assisting their mothers by tending siblings, carrying water, collecting firewood, herding small animals, weeding fields, or selling wares in the marketplace. Another is the expectation that once they are married, the gains from their productivity will benefit their husband's family. In parts of Africa, for instance, the payment of a bride price, whereby a prospective husband "purchases" a woman's labor and the rights to her offspring, is widespread. In anticipation of marrying their daughters early and obtaining a good bride price, according to a report from Tanzania, "parents. . .view education for girls as a waste of time and resources." Similar views are held throughout South Asia.[21]

Increasing the level of literacy among women and girls will require a campaign to simultaneously make education more accessible while changing discriminatory traditions. Flexible class schedules during harvest season and other periods when girls' labor is in high demand by their families is one way to increase access. Providing separate facilities for boys and girls, and training more female teachers, may increase female school attendance in Muslim cultures, where the fear of exposing young girls to males of any age keeps many out of school.[22]

According to the World Bank, providing elementary education for the estimated 120 million school-age children not now in school around the world would cost roughly $50 each, or $6 billion per year. Providing literacy training for illiterate women who are beyond school age would require an additional estimated $2 billion annually.[23]

Reducing infant mortality is another essential step. It is rare for birth rates to drop sharply if infant mortality is high. Immunizing the 55 percent of the world's children not currently protected from diphtheria, measles, polio, and tuberculosis would cost only a few dollars a piece.

Training mothers in the oral rehydration therapy used to treat infants with diarrhea, in basic hygiene, and in the health advantages of breast-feeding is a modest undertaking, one that is already under way in many countries. Although immunization and the training of mothers is not by itself enough to reduce infant mortality rates to those of industrial nations, these efforts would markedly lower infant deaths.[24]

The experience of a quarter-century of publicly supported international family planning programs yields a sense of what successful national efforts look like. The *State of World Population 1991* observes that "they have in common the support of political and social leaders at all levels; a wide choice of modern, safe, highly effective methods; well trained and highly motivated workers, with a sense of their value to the community and a respect for the community's own values; and the acceptance of the community at large."[25]

Even when family planning services are available, when literacy is high, and when infant mortality rates are falling, as they have been in East Asia for example, birth rates may not fall quickly enough. In these circumstances, governments sometimes turn to financial incentives. Indeed, incentives have played a part in several of the East Asian countries that have quickly lowered fertility, such as China, Singapore, South Korea, and Thailand, telescoping into a matter of years the fertility decline that was spread over many generations in western industrial countries.[26]

Governments have offered a wide array of incentives to couples to limit family size, but those that improve welfare seem to work best. South Korea offered free medical care and educational allowances to those couples agreeing to have only two children. Singapore gave small families preferred access to housing. Financial incentives that can be used to provide the old-age security once sought in large numbers of children are invariably among the more successful inducements. For example, China's Sichuan province makes monthly payments to couples who agree to have only one child.[27]

Some governments have linked family planning and local development by rewarding communities that achieve certain goals. Indonesia, aided by $3 million of World Bank financing, pioneered this approach. Financing the building of a new school, providing a pump for the village well, building a road to the village, or investing in other facilities that improve life for the villagers proved highly popular, spurring local communities to reach or even exceed their family planning goals.[28]

In a sustainable world, information will be widely available on the relationship between family size decisions and the environmental, economic, and social consequences of the resulting population growth rates. The starting point for an effective national population education program is thus a careful look into the future, a set of alternative projections that relate varying rates of population growth to environmental support systems and economic trends. Only when the three are combined can a useful view of the future be gained. Only then do our population policy choices become clear.

II

Instruments
of Change

8

From Growth to Sustainable Progress

Being able to visualize a sustainable world is the first step toward building one. Part I of this book sketched out new directions in energy, transportation, forestry, agriculture, and other resource areas that will enable our economy to become ecologically sound. The question then becomes, how do we get there? How can we shape a society that does not destroy the natural resources and environmental systems on which it depends?

Meeting that challenge requires profound political, social, and economic reforms involving all major segments of human activity—including businesses, religious organizations, civic groups, activists, governments, and voters. If successful, the struggle for a sustainable world will transform many facets of society, from politics and economics to cultural values and human rights.

The rising number of citizens around the world voicing concern about the fate of the earth promises to be the most forceful agent of change. (See Chapter 13.) Groups of farmers, women, environmental activists, and laborers of all kinds, in addition to individuals in many other walks of life, understand something governments and development agencies have been slow to grasp: human progress is a much broader concept than economic growth. The men and women in the vanguard of this historic transition are making clear that people's involvement in decision making—participatory democracy in the fullest sense—is one prerequisite for bettering the human condition.[1]

Movement toward sustainable patterns of energy use, food production, forestry, and demography raises far-reaching social questions. Equity, often viewed as merely an adjunct to economic growth, is an essential goal in its own right in a world striving to satisfy basic needs while protecting the environment. In many countries, for instance, without more equitable distribution of land, sustainable farming and forestry practices will not spring forth. And without justice being served to the countless indigenous peoples struggling to preserve their traditions and homelands, protection of the earth's biological richness, not to mention its cultural diversity, will be impossible.

Raising the status of women, whose freedoms are tightly circumscribed by social and cultural norms, is a key element of progress, in addition to being a moral imperative. As farmers, educators, family providers, and bearers of children, women will only achieve their fullest potential when accorded the same rights as men to shape their destinies. Further, they will limit their family size only when social and economic conditions allow them to do so without great material or psychological sacrifice, and when family planning programs begin to meet reproductive health needs as women themselves perceive them.[2]

Along with such political and social changes, economic systems will require a radical overhaul. Like an autoimmune disease, in which a body's own defense system attacks healthy tissue, our economy is assaulting the very life-support systems that keep it functioning. A fundamental restructuring of the rules and practices that shape economic activity is needed to stem this self-destruction. It is the nature of this transformation that the next few chapters focus on—in particular, the role of government incentives, tax policy, development aid, and debt relief in shaping a more sustainable world.

At the heart of this economic transition is the replacement of growth with sustainable progress as the central aim of political leaders and economic planners. The vast scale and rapid expansion of the global economy are hailed as great achievements of our time. With an annual output of $20 trillion, the world now produces in 17 days what it took an entire year to generate in 1900. Listening to most economists and politicians, unlimited growth of the economy seems not only possible but desirable. They tout growth in the gross national product as the answer to unemployment, poverty, ailing industries, fiscal crises, and myriad other societal ills. To question the wisdom of unlimited growth seems almost blasphemous, so ingrained is it in popular thinking about how the world works.[3]

Yet to agree that creating an environmentally sustainable economy is necessary is to acknowledge that limits on some forms of growth are inevitable—in particular, the consumption of physical resources. Textbook models often portray the economy as a self-contained system, with money flowing between consumers and businesses in a closed loop. In reality, however, the economy is not isolated. It operates within the boundaries of a global ecosystem with finite capacities to produce fresh water, form new topsoil, and absorb pollution. As a subset of the biosphere, the economy cannot outgrow its physical limits and remain intact.[4]

One useful measure of the economy's size relative to the earth's life-supporting capacity is the share of the planet's photosynthetic product now devoted to human activity. "Net primary production" is the amount of solar energy fixed by green plants through photosynthesis minus the energy used by those plants themselves. It is, in essence, the planet's total food resource—the biochemical energy that supports all forms of animal life, from earthworms to humans.

Biologist Peter Vitousek of Stanford University and his colleagues estimate that 40 percent of the earth's annual net primary production on land now goes directly to meet human needs or is indirectly used or destroyed by human activity—leaving 60 percent for the millions of other land-based species with which humans share the planet. While it took all of human history to reach this point, the share could double to 80 percent by 2030 if current rates of population growth continue; rising per capita consumption could shorten the doubling time considerably. Along the way, with people usurping an ever larger share of the earth's life-sustaining energy, natural systems will unravel faster. Exactly when vital thresholds will be crossed irreversibly is impossible to say. But as Vitousek and his colleagues state, those "who believe that limits to growth are so distant as to be of no consequence for today's decision makers appear unaware of these biological realities."[5]

For humanity to avoid the wholesale breakdown of natural systems requires not just a slowing in the expansion of our numbers but less resource-intensive ways of meeting our needs, such that human betterment does not come at the expense of future generations. The first and easiest phase in the transition is to increase greatly the efficiency with which water, energy, and materials are used, as described in earlier chapters, which will allow people's needs to be satisfied with fewer resources and less environmental harm. This shift is already under way, but is proceeding at a glacial pace compared with what is needed.

One example of the necessary approach can be found in California. Pioneering energy policies there have fostered utility investments in improved energy efficiency, causing electricity use per person to decline 0.3 percent between 1978 and 1988, compared with an 11-percent increase in the rest of the United States. Californians suffered no drop in living standards as a result; indeed, their overall welfare improved since their electricity bills were trimmed and their cooking, lighting, and other electrical needs were met with less sacrifice of air quality.[6]

Producing goods and services efficiently and with the most environmentally benign technologies available will move societies a long way toward sustainability, but it will not allow them to achieve it. Continuing growth in material consumption—the number of cars and air conditioners, the amount of paper used, and the like—will eventually overwhelm gains from efficiency, causing total resource use (and all the corresponding environmental damage) to rise. A halving of pollution emissions from individual cars, for example, will not result in much improvement in air quality if the total distance driven doubles, as it has in the United States since 1965.[7]

This aspect of the transition from growth to sustainability is thus far more difficult, as it goes to the heart of people's consumption patterns. In poorer countries, simply meeting the basic needs of growing human numbers will require that consumption of water, energy, and forest products increases, even if these resources are used with the utmost efficiency. But the dozen industrial countries that have stabilized their population size—including Germany, Hungary, Italy, and the United Kingdom—are in the best position to begin satisfying their needs with no net degradation of the natural resource base. These countries could be the first to benefit from realizing that some growth costs more than it is worth, and that an economy's optimum size is not its maximum size.[8]

Abandoning growth as an overriding goal does not mean forsaking the poor. Rising incomes and material consumption are essential to improving well-being in much of the Third World. But contrary to what political leaders imply, global economic growth as currently measured is not the solution to poverty. Despite the fivefold rise in world economic output since 1950, 1.2 billion people—more than ever—live in absolute poverty today. More growth of the sort engineered in recent decades will not save the poor; only a new set of priorities can.[9]

Formidable barriers stand in the way of shifting from growth to real progress as the central goal of economic policy. The vision that growth conjures up of an expanding pie of riches is a powerful and convenient political tool because it allows the tough issues of income inequality and skewed wealth distribution to be avoided. People assume that as long as there is growth, there is hope that the lives of the poor can be bettered without life-style changes by the rich. The reality, however, is that achieving an environmentally sustainable global economy is not possible without the fortunate limiting their consumption in order to leave room for the poor to increase theirs.

Movement toward a sustainable world thus requires practical economic reforms at both the national and international levels. With mounting evidence that environmental degradation and economic decline feed on each other, the fate of the poor and the fate of the planet have become tightly entwined. Redirecting the forces that are shaping prospects in developing countries today—including their heavy debt burdens and the tens of billions of dollars of development assistance they receive—is essential, as discussed in Chapter 12.

At the national level, a key challenge is to go beyond regulation as the primary approach to environmental protection. To be sure, regulations have reduced damage from air and water pollution, pesticides, toxic contamination, and other environmental ills in many cases. But unsustainable growth in all sectors—energy, transportation, industrial production, and agriculture—is far outpacing the ability of environmental laws and regulations to protect natural systems.

Many industrial nations now spend 1–2 percent of their total economic output on pollution control, and these figures are projected to increase in the years ahead. Such large sums spent on capturing pollutants at the end of the pipe are to some extent a measure of the economy's failure to foster practices that curb pollution at its source. Governments mandate catalytic converters for cars, but neglect energy-efficient public transport systems that would lessen dependence on the automobile. They require expensive methods of treating hazardous waste, while doing little to encourage industries to reduce their generation of such material.[10]

Of the many tools governments can use to reorient economic behavior, environmental taxes are among the most promising. (See Chapter 11.) Designed to make prices better reflect true costs, they would help ensure that those causing environmental harm pay for it, rather than society as a whole. In addition, eliminating government incentives that unwittingly foster resource destruction and establishing ones that encourage environmentally sound practices is essential to moving national economies quickly onto a stable path. (See Chapter 10.)

Despite what leading economic indicators may imply, no economy can be called successful if its prosperity comes at the expense of future generations and if the ranks of the poor continue to swell. We now face the wrenching question of whether the world our children inherit will provide for their needs as well as it does our own. Never before have policymakers had to be so concerned about future generations. A wholly new set of goals has been added to the traditional ones of creating jobs, spurring growth, and allocating resources efficiently.

9

Better Indicators
of Human Welfare

Just as a report card gauges a student's performance in various areas of study, so governments and citizens need indicators of their progress toward the goals they have set as a society. Today, the single most widely used indicator is the gross national product (GNP). A measure of the total output of goods and services in an economy, the GNP is the basis for ranking countries from rich to poor. Almost universally, a climbing GNP is taken to mean that a country's health is improving—and that its people are becoming better off.

But a closer look at the accounting system used to produce the GNP shows major failings in its ability to assess long-term progress. A country's economic book-keeping consists of income accounts, which when tallied produce the GNP figure, and capital accounts, which track changes in wealth. As lumber factories, textile mills, office buildings, and other artifacts age and fall into disrepair, something is subtracted from the capital accounts to reflect their depreciation in value. No similar subtraction is made, however, for the deterioration of forests, soils, air quality, and other natural endowments. Natural wealth of all kinds is whittled away with no record of the loss appearing in the national accounts.[1]

When trees are cut and sold for timber, for example, the proceeds are counted as income, and thus added to the GNP. But no debit is noted for the deterioration of the forest, an economic asset that if managed well could provide revenue long into the future. The result is an inflated sense of both income and wealth, creating the illusion that a country is better off than it really is and can sustain higher levels of consumption than is actually possible. As economist Robert Repetto of the World Resources Institute points out, this failure to distinguish between natural asset destruction and income generation makes the GNP "a false beacon, and can draw those who steer by it onto the rocks."[2]

Most in danger of running aground are developing countries whose economies remain closely tied to primary resources—fuels, timber, minerals, and agricultural crops. Bolivia, Colombia, Ethiopia, Ghana, Indonesia, Kenya, and Nigeria are among the countries that depend on primary products for 75 percent or more of their exports.[3]

Nigeria is an example of a country that overspent its natural account. Once among the world's largest tropical log exporters, the country's timber shipments fell off dramatically after many years of overcutting forests. In 1988, Nigeria earned only $6 million from forestry exports while spending $100 million on forest product imports. During the period of rapid logging, Nigeria's accounts failed to warn of the impending downturn. Indeed, a country can be headed toward ecological bankruptcy and still register GNP growth.[4]

Repetto and his colleagues have examined the implications for one resource-based economy, Indonesia, of a more accurate measure of income and wealth. Taking into account the depletion of just three natural resources—forests, soils, and petroleum—the researchers found the average annual growth in Indonesia's GNP from 1971 to 1984 dropped from 7.1 percent to 4 percent. If the exploitation of coal, mineral ores, and other nonrenewable resources had been included, along with the deterioration of fisheries and other renewable assets, the drop would have been even steeper.[5]

Besides being blind to the destruction of natural wealth, the GNP as currently calculated has another major failing: it counts as income many of the expenditures made to combat pollution and its adverse consequences. The Alaskan oil spill of March 1989, probably the most environmentally damaging accident in U.S. history, actually created a rise in the GNP, since much of the $2.2 billion spent on labor and equipment for the cleanup was added to income. Equally perverse, the medical care portion of the tens of billions of dollars in health costs incurred by Americans annually as a result of air pollution is counted on the plus side of the national income ledger.[6]

Although the nation certainly would be better off had the Alaskan oil spill never happened and if people did not suffer respiratory ailments from air pollution, the GNP suggests otherwise. As Frank Bracho of the South Commission Office in Venezuela puts it, this indicator "is an indiscriminate ensemble that assigns a positive value to any economic activity, be it productive, unproductive or destructive."[7]

As environmental deterioration accelerates, the discrepancy between the GNP's measure of progress and actual human well-being is widening. Indeed, the GNP becomes an obsolete measure of progress in a society striving to meet people's needs as efficiently as possible and with the least damage to the environment. What counts is not growth in output, but the quality of services rendered. Bicycles and light rail, for instance, are less resource-intensive forms of transportation than automobiles are, and contribute less to GNP. Yet a shift to mass transit and cycling for most passenger trips would enhance urban life by eliminating traffic jams, reducing smog, and making cities safer for pedestrians.

Likewise, investing in water-efficient appliances and irrigation systems instead of building more dams and diversion canals would meet water needs with less harm to the environment. Since massive water projects consume more resources than efficiency investments do, GNP would tend to decline. But quality of life would improve. It becomes clear that striving to boost GNP is often inappropriate and counterproductive. As ecologist and philosopher Garrett Hardin puts it, "For a statesman to try to maximize the GNP is about as sensible as for a composer of music to try to maximize the number of notes in a symphony."[8]

Recalculating the GNP so that it takes account of the depletion and deterioration of forests, fisheries, water supplies, air quality, and other natural assets is a critical first step toward bridging the growing gap between illusory and real economic gains. Some initiatives in this direction are under way. Australia, Canada, France, the Netherlands, and Norway are among the countries that have begun compiling inventories of their natural resources, a prerequisite to making the needed accounting adjustments. And the U.N. Statistical Commission, now in the process of revising its system of national accounts (which most market economies use), is expected to include guidelines for incorporating environmental damages into national accounting procedures when it issues its next "Blue Book" in 1993. But since the traditional approach to figuring the GNP will still be deemed acceptable, no widespread improvement in its reliability seems likely any time soon.[9]

Growing realization of the failings of the conventional GNP and income as the primary indicators of economic progress has led to the development of alternative yardsticks. Two interesting recent efforts are the Human Development Index (HDI) devised by the United Nations Development Programme and the Index of Sustainable Economic Welfare (ISEW) developed by economist Herman Daly and theologian John Cobb. A third indicator, per capita grain consumption, is a useful measure of changes in well-being in low-income countries, where the data needed to calculate the more sophisticated indices are typically not available on an annual basis.[10]

The Human Development Index, measured on a scale of 0 to 1, is an aggregate of three indicators: longevity, knowledge, and the command over resources needed for a decent life. For longevity, the U.N. team uses life expectancy at birth. For knowledge, they use adult literacy and mean years of schooling. And for the command over resources, they use gross domestic product (GDP) per person after adjusting it for purchasing power. Because these indicators are national averages, they do not deal directly with inequalities in wealth distribution, but by including longevity and literacy they do reflect indirectly the distribution of resources. A high average life expectancy, for example, indicates broad access to health care and adequate supplies of food and safe drinking water.[11]

A comparison of countries ranked by both per capita gross domestic product (adjusted for purchasing power) and HDI reveals some wide disparities. Costa Rica ranks 40th in the HDI, while South Africa, with an adjusted per capita GDP 27 percent higher than Costa Rica's, comes in at number 57. Despite their lower average purchasing power, Costa Ricans boast an adult literacy rate of 92 percent, compared with only 85 percent in South Africa, and at birth can expect to live 13 years longer than a newly born South African. Argentina, Chile, Poland, and Yugoslavia are among the other countries exhibiting high human development with comparatively modest per capita income.[12]

The HDI is still evolving; indeed, the country rankings published in 1991 differ markedly in some cases from those in 1990, the first year of the index, because of refinements made by the U.N. team. As more data become available, the HDI will begin to capture other determinants of human development as well. For example, enough information already exists in 30 countries to include sex inequalities in the HDI. When this is done, top-ranked Japan drops to number 17, while Finland, where women have rights and economic opportunities comparable to men's, moves up from 13 to number 1. Similarly, an HDI sensitive to the distribution of income has been calculated for 53 countries that could provide the needed data; again, the rankings change when this important factor is included.[13]

While the HDI represents a distinct improvement

over income figures as a measure of human well-being, it so far says nothing about environmental degradation. As a result, the HDI can rise through gains in literacy, life expectancy, or purchasing power that are financed by the depletion of natural resources, setting the stage for a longer term deterioration in living conditions.

The Daly-Cobb Index of Sustainable Economic Welfare, on the other hand, is a more comprehensive indicator of well-being, taking into account not only average consumption but also distribution and environmental degradation. To date, it has only been calculated for the United States. After adjusting the consumption component of the index for distributional inequality, the authors factor in several environmental measures, such as depletion of nonrenewable resources, loss of farmland from soil erosion and urbanization, loss of wetlands, and the cost of air and water pollution. They also incorporate what they call "long-term environmental damage," a figure that attempts to take into account such large-scale changes as the effects of global warming and of damage to the ozone layer.[14]

Applying this comprehensive measure shows a rise in welfare per person in the United States of some 42 percent between 1950 and 1976. (See Figure 9–1.) But after that the ISEW began to decline, falling by just over 12 percent by 1988, the last year for which it was calculated. Simply put, about 15 years ago the net benefits associated with economic growth in the United States fell below the growth of population, leading to a decline in individual welfare.[15]

The principal weakness of the ISEW is its dependence on information that is available in only a handful of nations. For example, few developing countries have comprehensive data on the extent of air and water pollution,

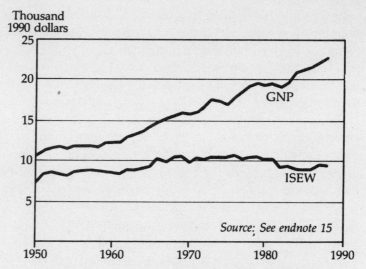

FIGURE 9-1. *Per Capita GNP and Index of Sustainable Economic Welfare, 1950-88*

not to mention measurements of year-to-year changes. The same drawback applies to the HDI, since life expectancy data depend heavily on infant mortality information that, astonishing as it may seem, is collected at best once a decade in most of the Third World.

Per capita grain consumption, however, is a useful measure of well-being in low-income countries that can be tracked on a yearly basis. This indicator captures the satisfaction of a basic human need, since people cannot survive if annual grain consumption falls much below 180 kilograms (about 1 pound a day) for an extended period. It is also less vulnerable to distortion by inequities of income and wealth. While the distribution of wealth between the richest and poorest one fifth of a population can be as great as 20 to 1, as indeed it is in

Algeria, Brazil, and Mexico, per capita consumption of grain by these same groups will not vary by more than 4 to 1.[16]

One drawback with this indicator is that it says nothing about how much of the grain consumed was produced unsustainably—by eroding soils, depleting water supplies, and the like. Another is that at some point, higher per capita grain consumption starts to imply a deterioration in human well-being rather than an improvement. Toward the top end of the scale people are consuming fat-rich livestock products known to increase heart disease and colon, breast, and other types of cancer, leading to an overall reduction in life expectancy. Per capita grain consumption is therefore best used as an indicator of well-being only in poorer countries.[17]

In the end, the search for the ideal indicator may prove as elusive as the legendary holy grail. Just as a doctor checks blood pressure, the kidneys' functioning, and many other vital signs to determine a person's overall health, so a basket of measures may be needed to accurately gauge human welfare. Collectively these indicators would provide feedback on how well society is doing in meeting its sustainability goals—including people's participation in decision making, wealth distribution, the status of women, and ecological stability. As economic analyst Hazel Henderson observes, "Only transparent and tangible indicators that people can readily understand and visualize and relate to their own lives will produce the desired political constituency for needed government policies."[18]

An indicator's relevance depends as much on how it is used as how it is constructed. The GNP has taken on a life of its own, having been granted an importance greatly out of line with what it is capable of measuring.

New indicators focused on sustainability criteria will prove valuable only if they are publicized and used by citizens' groups, the media, governments, and development agencies.

Routine reporting in U.S. cities of an air quality index provides an example of how a new measure can influence our assessment of well-being. A sunny, mild day with good air quality gives us a greater sense of satisfaction than one with air reported to be unhealthy. Prior to the use of this indicator, there was no way the average citizen could systematically track the important goal of breathing healthy air.

By the same token, if deforestation rates, carbon emissions, illnesses and deaths from unclean drinking water, and other measures of well-being were reported more routinely, our ability to judge how well off we are would greatly improve. Equally important, we would have the information needed to better set priorities for political action and social change.

10

Reshaping
Government Incentives

In most countries, government policy is a tortuous maze of incentives and disincentives designed to achieve certain ends—be they economic, social, or political. Unfortunately, and rather surprisingly, many government initiatives are stacked squarely against sustainability. Subsidies for road building, biased utility regulation, underpriced irrigation services, and below-cost timber sales are but a sampling of the numerous public programs that result in environmental damage. Collectively, governments spend tens of billions of dollars a year supporting environmentally unsound economic practices.

Subsidies for pesticides, which take such forms as tax exemptions and below-cost sales by government-controlled distributors, provide one example of these perverse incentives. In examining policies among nine developing countries—three each in Asia, Africa, and Latin America—Robert Repetto of the World Resources Institute in Washington, D.C., found pesticide subsidies in the early eighties ranging from 19 percent of the unsubsidized retail cost (in China) to 89 percent (in Senegal). In Egypt, subsidies equal to 83 percent of full retail costs drained the treasury of more than $200 million per year. The Egyptian government spent more per capita on pesticide subsidies in 1982 than it currently spends on health.[1]

By keeping pesticide costs low, governments aim to help farmers reduce pest damage and thereby increase crop yields. But the practice also encourages the excessive use of these agricultural supplements, increasing the number of chemical-related deaths and illnesses and releasing more pollutants into the environment. Moreover, subsidies inhibit the development and use of integrated pest management, which makes use of natural predators of pests, different planting patterns, pest-resistant crop varieties, and other nonchemical controls to stabilize and even increase harvests while minimizing hazards to health and the environment.[2]

Similarly, forests have suffered in rich and poor countries alike from government efforts to "develop" their economies and promote growth. Many governments are in effect subsidizing wholesale forest destruction, besides costing public treasuries vast sums each year. Laden with debt and looking for quick revenues, many tropical-country governments—often aided by international donors—have instituted tax credits and other fiscal incentives to encourage the conversion of forests to pasture, cash crops, and other land uses that may earn short-term profits but that rarely prove sustainable on poor tropical soils. Harvesting contracts excessively favorable to loggers have fueled "timber booms" that not only deplete and degrade forests but give colonizing farmers access to lands with soils that often will not sustain agriculture.[3]

Brazil, Indonesia, and the Philippines are among the countries losing from $500 million to more than $1 billion annually through such economic policies. Much of the deforestation of the Brazilian Legal Amazon, now totaling over 41 million hectares (an area slightly larger than Japan) can be linked to government road building, resettlement schemes, and various fiscal and land tenure policies. One particularly powerful incentive was hefty income tax credits—up to 50 percent in some cases—if the resulting savings were invested in the Amazon region. A good deal of this money went into clearing land to plant pasture for livestock ranches, many of which now yield only a small fraction of planned production; some no longer produce anything at all.[4]

Recent trends in Brazil suggest that removing such government inducements can help slow deforestation. In 1988 president José Sarney suspended most tax credits that encouraged forest clearing, and the administration of Fernando Collor de Mello has curtailed them further. Satellite data show that deforestation in the Amazon peaked in 1987 (though the widely reported loss of 8 million hectares for that year is now considered high), and then dropped in subsequent years, falling to 2.6 million hectares in 1989, and to 1.8 million in 1990. While a rainy dry season in 1989 and general economic malaise helped slow deforestation's pace, José Goldemberg, Brazil's Secretary of State for Science and Technology, credits at least part of the slowdown to stepped-up enforcement against illegal

burning and the elimination of the subsidies to
Amazonian farming and ranching projects. Reports that
some of the subsidies had been, or would soon be, rein-
stated were rebuffed by President Collor in June 1991,
when he promised to abolish them completely.[5]

In addition to yielding immediate environmental benefits, reducing such subsidies often lessens a source of
social inequity and frees up funds for programs that benefit the poor. The stipends in place today often enrich
the politically powerful and relatively well-off, who can
successfully lobby for economic favors. Pesticide and
irrigation subsidies, for instance, do nothing for the
cash-poor, dryland farmer who has no access to these
inputs. Likewise, support for cattle ranching and logging
bypasses those on the lower economic rungs.[6]

Eliminating incentives that promote resource destruction is common sense for an economy striving to
become environmentally sustainable. Reshaping economies rapidly enough to avoid the breakdown of vital life-
support systems, however, requires a distinctly different
set of policies—ones that accentuate the positive rather
than just eliminate the negative. Such incentives reward
ecologically sound practices, thereby making them attractive. They would not remain in place indefinitely,
but would jump-start the economy toward a sustainable
track.

There is almost no limit to the innovative ways of
marshaling private investment to work for the good of
the environment. But it demands a systematic look at
how current rules, regulations, and incentives shape behavior, and how they can be changed to foster sound
decisions.

In the United States, for example, the Conservation
Reserve Program gives farmers a financial reason to conserve soil. By agreeing to plant their most erodible land

in trees or grass for 10 years, farmers receive about $120 per hectare in annual rental payments. As of 1990, almost 14 million hectares had entered the five-year-old program, and excessive soil erosion nationwide had been cut by more than one third, from 1.6 billion tons to 1.0 billion.[7]

Reforming the way utilities are regulated could unleash the vast money-saving potential of energy efficiency while slowing global warming, reducing acid rain, and curbing urban air pollution. Under most current regulations, utility profits rise in tandem with electricity sales. Even though utilities could save energy— for example, through consumer service programs that install efficient lighting, low-flow showerheads, and insulation in homes and offices—at far less cost than supplying more, they have little incentive to do so.[8]

New programs in California, New York, Oregon, and five New England states are attempting to tackle this problem. They are "decoupling" profits from power sales, and giving utilities a direct financial incentive to invest in efficiency. In California, a proposal by the three largest electric utilities approved in August 1990 by the Public Utilities Commission ties earnings to energy savings. If conservation targets are met, one utility will be allowed electricity rates that yield an annual return of 14.6 percent on its conservation investments, substantially higher than the 10.7 percent the company would get from investing those funds in a new power plant. The other two will receive in profits 15–17 percent of the value of the energy savings they undertake for customers. Together, the efficiency programs will cost an estimated $500 million over the next two years, but are expected to save more than twice that in reduced power needs.[9]

Per capita energy use in developing countries is far

less than in industrial ones; in many cases, increased supplies are essential to raising living standards. But efficiency improvements have an enormous untapped potential here as well. Energy analyst Howard Geller has found, for instance, that over the next two decades Brazil could cut its growth in electricity use in half, from 5.2 percent per year to 2.6 percent, by promoting efficient technologies. Indeed, by using economic incentives to encourage conservation and efficiency investments—instead of subsidizing energy use—developing countries could avoid more than $1.4 trillion in energy supply costs over the next 20 years, saving scarce capital and improving the environment at the same time.[10]

Creative incentives could also give a much-needed boost to family planning efforts in the Third World, which regrettably have been neglected during the eighties. Setting up education savings accounts for the children of couples who limit their family size, reducing taxes for couples with no more than two children, and providing free family planning services are but a few of the forms of support possible.[11]

Well-designed incentive programs in this area are cost-effective, since expenditures to reduce fertility levels avoid larger social service costs later on. In Mexico, for example, every peso spent on family planning by the urban social security system between 1972 and 1984 saved nine pesos that would have been spent on maternal and infant health care. By providing nearly 800,000 women with contraceptives, the program averted 3.6 million unwanted births and resulted in a net savings of some 318 billion pesos ($2 billion).[12]

Until recently, relatively little attention has been given to the environmental effects of trade policies. With several important international trade deliberations under way, however, interest in sorting out the connections has surged over the past year. Trade rules and agreements are a major determinant of how natural resources are used, what pressures are placed on the environment, and who benefits from the huge money flows—now $3 trillion annually—that cross borders with the exchange of goods.[13]

From the standpoint of economic efficiency alone, trade distortions—including import quotas, tariffs, export subsidies, and domestic price supports—are undesirable, since they restrict competition in the global marketplace. It was a pre-world-war trading system plagued by such measures that spurred the creation of the General Agreement on Tariffs and Trade (GATT), which began operating in 1948 and now covers nearly 90 percent of world trade as traditionally measured. (The notion of trade is now expanding to include intellectual property and other money flows, but these are not counted in this figure.) Seven rounds of negotiations to amend the GATT have left many restrictions in place, particularly in politically sensitive areas such as agriculture. In recent years, the rich nations' trade barriers and domestic farm price supports for commodities such as sugar have cost the Third World an estimated $30 billion annually in lost agricultural income and industrial-country consumers some $245 billion in higher prices and taxes.[14]

Freer trade, however, would not necessarily help the poorest people in the Third World, nor be a net benefit to the environment. Much depends, for instance, on who gains from the added export revenue—peasant farmers or wealthy landowners. Much depends, too, on whether opening world markets would cause scarce land and water to be diverted from subsistence crops to export crops, at the expense of the poor and of food self-sufficiency.[15]

Moreover, some fear that freer trade could draw countries to the least common denominator in environmental protection and undermine conservation efforts. A proposal to "harmonize" international food safety standards under GATT could force countries with strict limits on pesticide residues to defend them before a GATT panel. The litigation costs and risk of losing create incentives to go no higher than the international standard. On the other hand, harmonization under GATT would likely result in stricter requirements in most developing countries, which now have low standards or none at all.[16]

Freer trade might also jeopardize the use of important conservation tools, such as the import ban placed on ivory to help protect the African elephant or the prohibition on raw log exports instituted by Indonesia, the Philippines, and Thailand to help preserve their forests. Unfortunately, as of May 1991, with the latest round of GATT negotiations extended because of differences over farm trade barriers, it appeared that negotiators had not seriously considered the environmental implications of their proposals.[17]

Similar issues arise with the accelerating integration of the European Community. For its members with more lax standards, such as Ireland, Portugal, and Spain, harmonized standards are having a salutary effect on the environment. The Community countries with the strictest standards, however, including Denmark, Germany, and the Netherlands, worry that their environmental gains will be eroded. NOAH, the Danish affiliate of Friends of the Earth, notes that "in Denmark we fear that the environmental standards we have been fighting for will be weakened as a result."[18]

Indeed, when the Danish government decided that all beer and soft drinks, whether produced domestically or imported, should be sold in returnable bottles, and that each bottle type be officially approved so as to ease refilling, it was taken to the European Court of Justice on the grounds that the requirement restricted free trade. Setting what appears to be a key precedent, the Court did not challenge Denmark's right to refuse imports of canned beverages and upheld on environmental grounds its right to require that all bottles be returnable. That the Danish initiative even was challenged, however, underscores the need to ensure that trade rules explicitly permit countries to set high standards and to freely pursue their environmental goals.[19]

The U.S.-Mexico free trade agreement now under negotiation raises equally complex issues. It could spur improvements in Mexico's environment provided U.S. and Mexican officials follow through on an environment plan to be negotiated alongside the trade agreement. Some environmentalists fear, however, that increased U.S. investment along the border zone will lead to more environmental damage no matter how stringently standards are set and enforced.[20]

In establishing a comprehensive incentive structure to promote sustainability, governments might now consider one overarching guideline: no net environmental damage. This would preclude projects that destroy forests, add carbon to the atmosphere, or pave over croplands unless additional investments were made to compensate for the damage done. For example, developers proposing to build a shopping mall that would destroy a parcel of woodland would need to reforest an equivalent area elsewhere. While obviously not a complete compensation, at least some of the ecological benefits of the original forest would be recaptured.

Applying this criterion to both public and private investors would ensure that those who profit from "development" plow some of their expected proceeds back into safeguarding the natural systems they place in jeopardy. It is no more radical a notion than that of requiring investors to pay back their creditors. In this case, the creditor is the global ecosystem.

11

Green Taxes

Many serious threats to humanity's future—from climate change and ozone depletion to air pollution and toxic contamination—arise largely from the economy's failure to value and account for environmental damage. Because those causing the harm do not pay the full costs, unsuspecting portions of society end up bearing them—often in unanticipated ways. People in the United States, for example, annually incur tens of billions of dollars in damages from unhealthy levels of air pollution, but car drivers pay nothing at the gas pump for their part in this assault. Similarly, if farmers pay nothing for using nearby waterways to carry off pesticide residues, they will use more of these chemicals than society would want, and rural people will pay the price in contaminated drinking water.[1]

Taxation is an efficient way to correct this shortcoming, and a powerful instrument for steering economies toward better environmental health. By taxing products and activities that pollute, deplete, or otherwise degrade natural systems, governments can ensure that environmental costs are taken into account in private decisions—whether to commute by car or bicycle, for example, or to generate electricity from coal or sunlight. If income or other taxes are reduced to compensate, leaving the total tax burden the same, both the economy and the environment can benefit.

Opinion polls show that a good share of the public thinks more should be spent on protecting the environment, but most people abhor the idea of higher taxes. By shifting the tax base away from income and toward environmentally damaging activities, governments can reflect new priorities without increasing taxes overall.[2]

So far, most governments trying to correct the market's failures have turned to regulations, dictating specifically what measures must be taken to meet environmental goals. This approach has improved the environment in many cases, and is especially important where there is little room for error, such as in disposing of high-level radioactive waste or safeguarding an endangered species. Taxes would be a complement to regulations, not a substitute.

Environmental taxes are appealing because they can help meet many goals efficiently. Each individual producer or consumer decides how to adjust to the higher costs. A tax on air emissions, for instance, would lead some factories to add pollution controls, others to change their production processes, and still others to redesign products so as to generate less waste. In contrast to regulations, environmental taxes preserve the strengths of the market. Indeed, they are what economists call corrective taxes: they actually improve the functioning of the market by adjusting prices to better reflect an activity's true cost.[3]

In a minor form, environmental or so-called green taxes already exist in many countries. A survey by the Organisation for Economic Co-operaton and Development turned up more than 50 environmental charges among 14 of its members, including levies on air and water pollution, waste, and noise, as well as various product charges, such as fees on fertilizers and batteries. In most cases, however, these tariffs have been set too low to motivate major changes in behavior, and have been used instead to raise a modest amount of revenue for an environmental program or other specific purpose. Norway's charge on fertilizers and pesticides, for instance, raises funds for programs in sustainable agriculture—certainly a worthy cause—but is too low to reduce greatly the amount of chemicals farmers use in the short term.[4]

There are, however, some notable exceptions. In the United Kingdom, a higher tax on leaded gasoline increased the market share of unleaded petrol from 4 percent in April 1989 to 30 percent in March 1990. And in late 1989, the U.S. Congress passed a tax on the sale of ozone-depleting chlorofluorocarbons (CFCs) in order to hasten their phaseout, which the nation has agreed to do by the end of the decade, and to capture the expected windfall profits as the chemicals' prices rise. The most widely used CFCs are initially being taxed at $3.02 per kilogram ($1.37 per pound), roughly twice the current price; the tax will rise to $6.83 per kilogram by 1995 and to $10.80 per kilogram by 1999. During the first five years, this is expected to generate $4.3 billion, which will be added to the government's general revenues.[5]

A comprehensive set of environmental taxes, designed as part of a broader restructuring of fiscal policy, could do much more to move economies quickly onto a sustainable path. Most governments raise the bulk of their revenues by taxing income, profits, and the value added to goods and services. These are convenient ways of collecting money, and ones that often serve an important redistributive function, but such taxes distort the economy by discouraging work, savings, and investment. Substituting taxes on pollution, waste, and resource depletion for a large portion of current levies could improve both the environment and the economy, and be done in a way that keeps the total tax structure equitable.

A comprehensive green tax code would alter economic activity in many areas. It would place fees on carbon emissions from the burning of coal, oil, and natural gas, and thereby slow global warming. It would penalize the use of virgin materials, and thus encourage recycling and reuse. It might, among other things, charge for the generation of toxic waste, and so foster waste reduction and the development of safer products, and for emissions of air pollutants, thus curbing acid rain and respiratory illnesses. And it might impose levies on the overpumping of groundwater, which would encourage more efficient water use.

An analysis of eight possible green taxes for the United States suggests that they can raise substantial revenues while working to protect the environment. (See Table 11–1.) Determining tax levels that reduce harm to human health and the environment without damaging the economy is complicated; the ones shown here are simply for illustration. Because some taxes have

TABLE 11-1. *United States: Potential Green Taxes*

Tax Description	Quantity of Taxed Activity	Assumed Charge[1]	Resulting Annual Revenue[2]
			(billion dollars)
Carbon content of fossil fuels	1.3 billion tons	$100 per ton	130.0
Hazardous wastes generated	266 million tons	$100 per ton	26.6
Paper and paperboard produced from virgin pulp	61.5 million tons	$64 per ton	3.9
Pesticide sales	$7.38 billion	half of total sales	3.7
Sulfur dioxide emissions[3]	21 million tons	$150 per ton	3.2
Nitrogen oxides emissions[3]	20 million tons	$100 per ton	2.0
Chlorofluoro-carbon sales[4]	225 million kilograms	$5.83 per kilogram	1.3
Groundwater depletion	20.4 million acre-feet	$50 per acre-foot	1.0

[1]Charges shown here are for illustration only, and are based simply on what seems reasonable given existing costs and prices. In some cases several taxes would exist in a given category to reflect differing degrees of harm; the hazardous waste tax shown, for instance, would be the average charge. [2]Since revenue would diminish as the tax shifted production and consumption patterns, and since some taxes have multiple effects, the revenue column cannot be added to get a total revenue estimate. [3]The Clean Air Act passed in October 1990 requires utility sulfur dioxide emissions to drop by 9 million tons and nitrogen oxide emissions by 1.8 million tons by the end of the decade. [4]This tax already exists. Revenues shown here are expected for 1994.

SOURCE: Worldwatch Institute. See endnote 6 for sources on the quantity of taxed activity.

multiple effects (a carbon tax for example, would lower both carbon and sulfur dioxide emissions by discouraging fossil fuel consumption) and because the taxed activities will decline even before taxes are fully in place, revenues shown in the table cannot be neatly totaled. But it seems likely that the eight levies listed here could raise on the order of $130 billion per year, allowing personal income taxes to be reduced about 30 percent.[6]

A team of researchers at the Umwelt und Prognose Institut (Environmental Assessment Institute) in Heidelberg proposed a varied set of taxes for the former West Germany that would have collectively raised more than 210 billion deutsche marks ($136 billion). The researchers analyzed more than 30 possible "eco-taxes," and determined tax levels that would markedly shift consumption patterns for each item. In some cases, a doubling or tripling of prices was needed to cut consumption substantially. Halving pesticide use, for example, would require a tax on the order of 200 percent of current pesticide prices.[7]

Phasing in each environmental tax over, say, 5 or 10 years would ease the economic effects and allow for a gradual adjustment. The tax on carbon emissions from fossil fuels is the one likely to raise the most revenue in most industrial countries. Levied on the carbon content of coal, oil, and natural gas, an effective charge must be high enough to reduce emissions of carbon dioxide, now the official goal of more than a dozen industrial nations. Carbon taxes went into effect in Finland and the Netherlands in early 1990; Sweden began collecting carbon taxes in January 1991. Unfortunately, none of these levies seems high enough to spur major changes in energy use. In the case of Sweden, however, a hefty sulfur dioxide tax, which also went into effect in January 1991, combined with the small carbon tax, may encourage measurable reductions in fossil fuel burning.[8]

In September 1990, the 12 environment ministers from the European Community (EC) gathered in Rome to discuss the possibility of Community-wide green taxes. Though they failed to reach agreement, the meeting placed environmental taxes squarely on Europe's political agenda. The EC Environment Commissioner, Carlo Ripa di Meana, himself supports a common EC tax on carbon emissions, as do Belgium, Denmark, France, and Germany. The less wealthy EC members fear, however, that a harmonized tax would be too high, jeopardizing their growth, while the Netherlands worries that it might be too low. Even if Community-wide taxes are not set, it seems likely that other countries will introduce them individually over the next few years.[9]

In the United States, energy tax proposals have languished in the Congress. With little support for energy efficiency and renewable sources coming from the Bush administration, all that Congress approved in 1990 was a 5¢-per-gallon increase in the federal gasoline tax. Such a meager additional charge will do little to discourage automobile use or reduce carbon emissions.[10]

Of all the energy taxes possible, that on carbon—levied on coal at the mine, on oil at the wellfield or dock, and on natural gas at the wellhead—would most efficiently and effectively reduce carbon dioxide (CO_2) emissions. An August 1990 study by the U.S. Congressional Budget Office (CBO) examined the effect of phasing in a carbon tax over the next decade, beginning with $11 per ton of carbon in 1991 and rising to $110 per ton in 2000 (in 1988 dollars). When fully implemented, the tax would generate an estimated $120 billion in revenues.[11]

The CBO estimates that the fee of $110 per ton of carbon would raise oil and natural gas prices by about half over the levels currently projected for 2000, and the expected price of coal—the most carbon-rich of the fossil fuels—by 256 percent. This would encourage industries and consumers to invest in efficiency measures and to switch to non-carbon energy sources.[12]

The model used by CBO that best reflects business and consumer responses to changed energy prices shows that CO_2 emissions would be 37 percent lower than now projected in the year 2000, while the nation's energy efficiency would improve by 23 percent. The nation would also meet the much discussed international target of cutting CO_2 emissions 20 percent from the 1988 level by the year 2005. The model projects a drop of $45 billion in the gross national product in 2000, a modest 0.6 percent, which could likely be avoided by pairing the carbon tax with reductions in income or other taxes.[13]

Completely shifting the tax base away from income and toward environmental concerns would not be desirable. Income taxes are usually designed to make the wealthy pay proportionately more; green taxes, on balance, would not serve this equity goal. Hefty carbon charges, for instance, would cause heating oil prices to rise, imposing a heavy burden on low-income households who spend a greater share of their income on this essential item. To offset this undesirable impact, income tax rates would need to be lowered even more for poorer people. Government payments could compensate the very poor, the elderly, and others who may not pay any income taxes at all now but who might experience higher living costs under an environmental tax code.

Another reason to blend income and environmental taxes is that green-tax revenues would diminish as production and consumption patterns shift away from taxed activities. Environmental levies would therefore not be as constant a source of revenue over time as income taxes are. Once businesses and consumers have adjusted to the new tax scheme, revenues from green taxes and income taxes would strike a more stable balance.

Besides their help in reshaping national economies, green taxes can also raise funds for global initiatives that require transfers from rich countries to poorer ones, including slowing global warming, preserving tropical forests and biological diversity, and protecting the ozone shield. Such transfers would serve as partial payment for the ecological debt industrial countries have incurred by causing most of the damage to the global environment thus far. An extra tax of $10 per ton of carbon emitted in industrial countries (excluding Eastern Europe and the Soviet Union) would initially generate $25 billion per year for a global fund.[14]

Reshaping fiscal policy to be an instrument of environmental restoration may be difficult at a time when policymakers are concerned with the economic slowdown in much of the world and with revitalizing the flagging economies of the former Soviet bloc. Yet nothing lasting will be gained by the continued pursuit of growth at the environment's expense.

12

Banking
on the Environment

After a decade of economic and environmental decline, many developing countries are at a dangerous crossroads. Unless they are able to invest sufficient resources in such things as conserving soil, improving energy efficiency, and providing family planning services, their life-support systems will be irreparably damaged. And as environmental problems become global in scale, the world as a whole has a growing stake in the ability to marshall an environmentally sustainable development effort in the Third World.

Restoring financial balance to the global economy is essential to putting societies on a sustainable path. By 1990, Third World debt had reached the staggering figure of $1.2 trillion, 44 percent of its collective gross national product (GNP). The cost of servicing that debt in 1990 was $140 billion, a burden that has contributed to a reversal of the traditional capital flow from rich countries to poor ones. The net hemorrhage from South to North now stands at more than $35 billion annually. Developing countries are not only unable to invest in their futures, they are forced to spend inordinate sums on debts accumulated as a result of capital-intensive projects that provided minimal benefits for their people.[1]

Lack of capital has in recent years made it all but impossible for developing countries to invest adequately in forest protection, soil conservation, irrigation improvements, more energy-efficient technologies, or pollution control devices. Even worse, growing debts have compelled them to sell off natural resources, often their only source of foreign currency. Like a consumer forced to hock the family heirlooms to pay credit card bills, developing countries are plundering forests, decimating fisheries, and depleting water supplies—regardless of the long-term consequences.

The economic development of the United States in the nineteenth century was largely financed with European investments. Likewise, the rapid postwar rebuilding of Europe would have been inconceivable without the large capital infusion of the U.S.-led Marshall Plan. For today's developing countries, with their enormous environmental problems, the challenge is greater, since they must build an economy that is sustainable as well as financially strong. Greatly lessening the debt burden is now a prerequisite for environmentally sustainable Third World development.

Today, very little of the aid money disbursed to developing countries by governments and international lending institutions supports ecologically sound development. The World Bank, the largest single funder, lacks a coherent vision of a sustainable economy, and its lending priorities often run counter to the goal of creating one. Bilateral aid agencies, with a few important exceptions, do little better. Moreover, the scale of total lending falls far short of that needed to help the Third World escape from the overlapping traps of poverty, overpopulation, and ecological decline.

Total nonmilitary aid provided by rich nations to poor ones in 1989 reached $41 billion. Loans from the World Bank and the regional development banks totaled $28 billion that year, most of it borrowed on commercial markets. For 20 nations, annual net receipts exceed one fifth of their individual GNPs. U.S. aid has actually declined in real terms, to $7.7 billion in 1989, while Japan has emerged as the world's largest donor, contributing nearly $9 billion. (See Table 12–1.) Measured as a share of GNP, the differences among aid levels are notable— from less than 0.2 percent in the United States to more than 1 percent in Norway.[2]

The Organisation for Economic Co-operation and Development has set a goal of boosting annual aid levels to 0.7 percent of each member's GNP, which would double current assistance to over $80 billion a year. Unfortunately, in many donor countries aid levels are declining. Moreover, the shift of aid toward such sustainable development priorities as reforestation, family planning, or energy efficiency is proceeding slowly if at all. Just 7 percent of bilateral funds go to population and health, for example.[3]

As much as two thirds of some countries' aid is tied to the purchase of goods and services, essentially a form of export promotion. Furthermore, the Soviet Union and the United States give most of their aid to just a handful

TABLE 12-1. *Development Assistance from Selected Industrial Nations, 1989*

Country	Development Aid	Share of GNP
	(billion dollars)	(percent)
Norway	0.92	1.04
Netherlands	2.09	0.94
France	7.45	0.78
Canada	2.32	0.44
Italy	3.61	0.42
Germany	4.95	0.41
Australia	1.02	0.38
Japan	8.95	0.32
United Kingdom	2.59	0.31
United States	7.66	0.15

SOURCE: See endnote 2.

of nations deemed strategically important. Moscow's aid is now dwindling rapidly, and Washington provides 39 percent of its nonmilitary aid to Israel, Egypt, and El Salvador, which together have only 1.2 percent of the world's population. Fortunately, other donor nations in Europe and elsewhere tend to spread their development assistance more widely.[4]

Aid programs are therefore badly in need of an overhaul. Norway, in many ways the world leader in development assistance, might serve as a model. Not only does this small nation provide more aid as a share of its GNP than any other country, it is increasingly focused on sustainable development, as mandated by Parliament in 1987. Agriculture and fisheries receive 19 percent of Norwegian development assistance, and education gets 8 percent. In addition, a special environment fund disbursed more than $10 million to developing countries in 1990. The leading recipients of Norwegian aid are the neediest countries—including, for example, Bangladesh, India, and Tanzania.[5]

If the world as a whole had the priorities reflected in Norway's aid budget, Third World environmental improvement would be much further along. One encouraging initiative is proposed legislation in the U.S. Congress that would make environmentally sustainable development a major aim of U.S. foreign aid.[6]

The World Bank and the three regional development banks are well situated to help Third World countries develop sustainably. Their influence is even greater than suggested by the $28 billion lent to developing nations in 1989. Their priorities are reflected in the lending patterns of commercial banks and in the investment decisions of many poor nations. A clearly articulated sustainable development strategy and a new set of investment priorities by the World Bank would provide badly needed leadership for the world.[7]

At the moment, the World Bank continues its traditional bread and butter lending for large capital-intensive projects such as road building, dam construction, and irrigation projects, making it an accomplice to the pollution of rivers, the burning of rain forests, and the strip-mining of vast areas, often in countries that cannot even monitor the damage. In many cases, Bank-supported projects are now the object of vehement opposition by local people—usually the rural poor, who are most affected.[8]

Officials respond to such criticism by noting that the Bank is first and foremost a lending institution, and that its priority is the financial viability of its loans. Indeed, the Bank prides itself on the fact that no nation has ever defaulted on one of its loans. However, even many bankers concede that the world has changed greatly in recent years, and that short-term financial thinking can be the road to long-run ruin.

Serious efforts to reform the Bank began slowly in the early eighties under pressure from environmental groups worldwide. In a 1987 speech, Bank president Barber Conable acknowledged the institution's problems and pledged new initiatives. This was followed by the creation of a central Environment Department as well as four regional environment divisions. Since then, environmental reports of every sort have flowed from the Bank. The 1992 *World Development Report*, the Bank's flagship document, is to be devoted to sustainable development issues.[9]

But at the working level, progress has been much slower. By late 1990, the professional environmental staff numbered just 54, assisted by 23 consultants—out of a total World Bank professional staff of more than 4,000. Among the achievements touted by Bank officials are 11 "freestanding" environmental loans in 1990. Some are indeed laudable, such as $237 million for sewerage, drainage, and water supply improvements in several Indonesian cities. Included, however, is a "sustainable forestry" project in Côte d'Ivoire that may result in accelerated logging and deforestation. Even more suspect is the Bank's claim that half its loans now include "environmental components." This classification is often little more than a new label on old projects.[10]

President Conable has found it easy to get inspiring reports written, but harder to motivate the people who continue to churn out loans for dams and roads. Bank staffers are rewarded for the quantity of loans they process, not their quality. The Bank is also plagued by a culture of secrecy and arrogance that makes it resistant both to its own internal reformers and to pressures exerted from the outside by governments and nongovernmental organizations (NGOs). Staff who push for faster and more fundamental reforms have sometimes been reassigned to less influential posts.[11]

Although new priorities, such as improved energy efficiency, are recommended in World Bank policy papers, they are still badly underfunded. Energy supply projects such as coal plants and hydro dams are the largest area of Bank lending, receiving 16–18 percent of the loans in recent years. Energy efficiency loans still represent less than 3 percent of the Bank's lending to energy and industry.[12]

An environmental assessment process has also been set up to review the potential impact of proposed projects. But its effectiveness is undermined by the fact that the borrowing countries, eager to obtain loans, are responsible for the assessment; often they have neither the staff nor the skills to do the job. As a result, destructive projects are still going forward with only minor restrictions.[13]

Part of the problem is that within this huge bureaucracy, the new Environment Department is weak—appended to the Policy, Research, and External Affairs complex, with no direct involvement in lending operations. The environmental review process will need to be more carefully controlled by in-house staff if the list of environmental disasters supported by the World Bank is to be shortened. The April 1991 appointment of a new Director provides an opportunity for the Department to be strengthened.[14]

It is time for a second generation of fundamental reforms at the World Bank—ones that address the institutional resistance to change and set genuinely new priorities. Even a strengthened Environment Department is not enough. Without a coherent vision of environmentally sustainable development, the Bank will continue to stumble from one environmental confrontation to another.

Restructuring lending programs will involve tackling some thorny issues. The World Bank's current portfolio of large, capital-intensive project loans requires less staff time to design and oversee than a program of smaller loans would. This allows the institution to finance its lending using the small margin between its own borrowing costs and the rate it charges developing countries—which is lower than comparable commercial lending rates. To support smaller, more labor-intensive projects such as community woodlots, integrated pest management for small farmers, rural cookstove industries, or urban bicycle factories, new financing mechanisms are needed.

One possibility is to shift the balance between project and policy lending. This latter category now accounts for 20–30 percent of the Bank's loan portfolio and is used to meet government funding needs, including structural adjustment lending that has been used recently to reduce subsidies and otherwise streamline Third World governments. Policy lending involves lower overhead costs than development loans do; if their share were increased, the project loans could be made at lower interest rates, making it possible to support smaller, more labor-intensive development efforts. At the same time, however, it is essential that policy loans be reoriented to encourage environmentally sound development, in effect using structural adjustment lending to foster environmental as well as economic reforms. Levying pollution taxes, for example, or cutting pesticide subsidies would improve the fiscal health of Third World governments and reduce their environmental problems.[15]

On the project lending side, an environmentally responsible development bank might, at least in the initial years, be one that provided more loans but less money. The Bank needs to emphasize the nature and effect of its loans rather than the dollars disbursed. It could support such projects as raising irrigation efficiency, building factories that turn out efficient light bulbs, and training workers in everything from planting trees to installing solar collectors. Directing even a small portion of loans to facilities such as Bangladesh's Grameen Bank, which makes "micro loans" to the rural poor, could spur myriad grassroots development projects.[16]

For sustainable development to become the priority, it is essential that the development banks do more to involve local people in decision making. This would require easing the oppressive secrecy that now prevents both the affected public and even the Bank's directors from learning essential details of proposed projects. Ideally, the World Bank would become a force for openness and provide avenues for public participation. Many groups in the Third World are able and willing to get involved in this process.[17]

Beyond the reform of aid and lending, debt reduction is essential to sustainable economic progress in developing countries. Although the first step out of the morass is for poor nations to embark on fundamental economic reforms, richer countries have their own responsibility to help reduce Third World debts, much of them accrued with their encouragement.

Unfortunately, efforts to date have just nibbled at the problem. Neither the Baker plan of the mid-eighties nor the Brady plan that followed has appreciably reduced the debt burden, though they did give the commercial banks breathing room to reduce their risk of default. The only instances in which large amounts of debt have been forgiven are when politics necessitated it. The Polish debt was halved in 1991 as a way of ensuring its pursuit of a market-based economic system, while Egypt's debt was slashed an equivalent amount in return for its supporting the U.S.-led coalition in the Persian Gulf War.[18]

Turning the debt crisis around will require more than rescheduling payments or issuing new loans. The international financial institutions and commercial banks that hold most of the outstanding notes will almost certainly need to write down many debts and entirely forgive others. The governments of Canada, Germany, the United Kingdom, and the United States have between them already forgiven more than $5 billion worth of public loans to sub-Saharan African countries—largely for humanitarian and practical economic reasons. This is the right approach, but commercial loans will also need to be gradually written off.[19]

A number of imaginative proposals to reduce Third World debt have been floated, but so far the leadership needed to implement them has been lacking. By definition, any successful debt-reduction strategy is one that brings Third World debt down to a level that allows environmentally sound development to be restored. Achieving this may require debt reduction on the order of 60 percent, a cut from $1.2 trillion to $500 billion.

Such a cut would be eminently feasible if it were undertaken gradually over a decade. (The $50 billion raised in a matter of months to finance the Gulf War is evidence of what can be accomplished when the need is urgent.) Indeed, without substantial debt reduction, the world financial system will continue to be at risk. As several economists have suggested, it is logical to build incentives for environmental protection into any debt-reduction strategy.[20]

On a more limited scale, U.S. biologist Thomas Lovejoy has introduced an environmental financing concept known as "debt-for-nature swaps." Under this scheme, a conservation organization buys a portion of a debtor's obligation from a commercial bank on the open market, usually at just 15–30 percent of its face value. The developing country's central bank then issues bonds in local currency, at something less than the value of the original debt, which are used by an indigenous environmental group for conservation purposes. For all the parties involved, these debt-for-nature swaps can be a win-win situation. By early 1991, 18 such swaps had been arranged in nine countries, including Bolivia, Madagascar, and Poland.[21]

The next step is to go beyond these kinds of limited loan swaps and begin writing off large amounts of Third World debt in exchange for the adoption of sustainable development programs. Such arrangements could spur far-reaching changes in Third World development paths, and ensure that new loans go into well-thought-out development efforts. If industrial-country governments and private banks were to adopt this approach widely, it would be possible to reduce debt significantly as well as provide billions of dollars to help more countries onto a more sustainable path.

An early example of this approach is the Dutch government's 1989 purchase of $33 million worth of Costa Rica's debt in exchange for $10 million of local investments in reforestation, watershed management, and soil conservation. In early 1991, the U.S. government announced a plan to exchange 10 percent of Poland's outstanding U.S. debts for an equivalent amount of local investments in environmental restoration. This initiative is likely to make some $350 million available for spending by a newly created foundation for the environment. In addition, the U.S. government hopes that other governments will follow its lead, increasing the total debt-for-environment deal to more than $1 billion.[22]

Another financing idea whose time has come is that of establishing an international environmental fund to provide resources to address global concerns such as climate change and ozone depletion that individual nations do not have sufficient incentive to cope with on their own. In 1990, the international community agreed to set up a Global Environmental Facility—managed by the World Bank in cooperation with the U.N. Development Programme and U.N. Environment Programme. Although the Bank's reputation for efficiency led governments to place the fund there, some environmental NGOs have opposed this, given the Bank's poor environmental record. As of mid-1991, the facility was off to a slow and rocky start.[23]

The money in the Global Environment Facility will go to poor nations that are short of capital for needed environmental investments. It is to be dedicated to four main areas: protecting the ozone layer, limiting greenhouse gas emissions, preserving biodiversity, and protecting international water resources. A fund of $1.4 billion has been established for the first three years, with plans to spend $273 million in 1991, supporting 15 environmental-protection projects and 11 technical assistance programs. Strengthening this fund and possibly establishing other financing mechanisms is on the agenda for the 1992 U.N. Conference on Environment and Development.[24]

Unless nations address the twin problems of growing Third World poverty and increasing international inequity, global economic and environmental decline are certain to accelerate. So far, however, the world community is making only halting progress in mobilizing the financial resources to stop the process of global environmental decline. The central issues are how to reduce the debt burden, how to increase and rechannel development aid, and how to overcome the institutional biases and inertia of the World Bank and other multilateral lenders.

III

The
Challenge
Ahead

13

The Struggle
for a New World

Building an environmentally sustainable economy could revolutionize nearly every facet of human existence. Like the agricultural or industrial revolutions that preceded it, the environmental revolution will lead inevitably to different economic, social, and political patterns. But the pace of change will be swifter than those earlier transformations. Whereas the agricultural revolution took several thousand years, and the industrial revolution spanned centuries, the transition to an ecologically secure world will have to be compressed into a few decades.

Achieving the goal of a sustainable society depends on redirecting the engine of "economic development" that has inexorably reshaped the globe during the past century. Although economic tools, such as those discussed in the preceding chapters, are essential instruments, they are unlikely to be effective unless accompanied by major political changes. Ultimately, the struggle for a livable world is about overcoming concentrations of economic power, about the universal human yearning for political freedoms, and about the fight for human rights and dignity. As long as any of these is systematically denied, the struggle is unlikely to succeed.

The transition to a new world will not be orderly or predictable. The needed economic and technological changes are themselves profound. But the social and political transformations are likely to be even more wrenching and difficult. Though it is tempting to think the prerequisites of a sustainable society can be decreed—two-child families or soil-conserving agriculture, for example—the actual process of change is far more complex. Population size is unlikely to stabilize without access to health care for women; likewise, fair distribution of land makes sustainable agriculture more feasible.

Addressing such issues requires a revolution at many levels—from local communities to global institutions. Grassroots groups, national governments, and international organizations all have roles to play in forging a sustainable society. Human institutions, many of which have been in place for decades or centuries, need to be reshaped in a matter of years.

Some of the most far-reaching changes are coming from the grassroots as individuals see their lives and their relationships with nature in a new light. As a result, they are making changes in their life-styles, and are insisting on changes in public policy. Environmental activism has swept the world in the past decade—from Sweden to Senegal, from Moscow to Manaus. Governments at every level are being pushed by thousands of citizens' groups to pursue environmental reforms.

In developing countries, the proliferation of grass-roots organizations has been extraordinary—a response to the failure of governments to cope with growing social and environmental problems. Their missions range from providing basic services to the poor, such as health care for women, to protecting the natural environments and livelihoods of rural people, as India's Chipko (tree hugger) movement or Kenya's Greenbelt organization has done. As Alan Durning wrote in a 1989 study, "These people understand global degradation in its rawest forms. To them, creeping destruction of ecosystems has meant lengthening workdays, failing livelihoods, and deteriorating health. And it has pushed them to act."[1]

No international agency charts the growth in grass-roots action the way it might trends in oil or grain production. But one thing is clear from the country studies and anecdotal information available: the surge in grass-roots activity—particularly among the poorest segments of today's societies—is a remarkable and vastly under-reported phenomenon. According to one estimate, more than 100,000 such organizations exist, with 100 million members in the Third World alone. The grinding, growing poverty and accompanying political instability in developing countries do not preclude serious concern about the environment. Arguably, they accentuate it.[2]

In the Philippines, a country with an annual per capita income of $680, the loss of the country's once verdant forests has forced environmental issues onto a crowded national agenda—led by grassroots organizations whose membership is estimated at 5 million. During the late eighties, for example, dozens of peasant organizations,

representing 1.5 million Filipinos, joined forces to promote a People's Agrarian Reform Code, a response to
the failure of the government's land reform efforts. It is
intended to abolish absentee landownership and to provide support to peasants who want to acquire land. The
idea is to encourage wide replication of the initiatives
pioneered by individual rural groups, including introduction of organic farming techniques and reforestation
of coastal mangroves.[3]

In Bangladesh, with a per capita income of just $160
per year, millions of rural poor are forced by a shortage
of arable land to live at sea level in areas where periodic
flooding is inevitable. The loss of more than 100,000
lives in the cyclone-related flooding of May 1991 was
just the latest in a series of environmental tragedies. But
while the international community focuses on emergency relief, Bangladesh's burgeoning grassroots movement is providing some answers to the country's most
intractable problems. The Proshika Centre for Human
Development, for instance, concentrates on alleviating
poverty in rural areas. Proshika has helped villagers use
hardy native seed varieties, relying on crop rotation and
the intercropping of rice, vegetables, and fruit trees. By
applying fewer chemical fertilizers and pesticides, the
farmers also save money. Proshika has spawned more
than 700 women's gardening groups, as well as an extensive roadside forestry program.[4]

Those who seek to protect the resources on which the
poor depend often must confront powerful political and
economic interests—from Brazil's armed forces to
India's influential construction industry. When dissent-
ers who challenge the status quo do not have their rights
guaranteed, they are often evicted from their lands,
threatened, or killed. The 1988 murder of Amazonian

rubber tapper leader Chico Mendes is but the most publicized of these tragic events. In Malaysia, activists who fought to protect the tropical forests of Sarawak have been jailed without trial for extended periods. Thus for environmental reform efforts to succeed, questions of political participation, freedom of information, land distribution, human rights, and empowerment of women must also be addressed.[5]

Coinciding with and in some cases flowing from the explosion in grassroots organizations are a plethora of citizens' democracy movements. In Eastern Europe, for example, the political revolutions of 1989 were preceded by a host of citizen actions, many provoked by environmental concerns, others tied to churches and human rights groups, but all demanding a say in governments that denied them access. In the Soviet Union, thousands of such organizations have arisen in the last few years, stimulating a multifaceted political dialogue.[6]

Around the world, the struggles for democratic expression and environmental sustainability are inextricably linked. To take one example, the destruction of the teak forests of Myanmar (formerly Burma)—the most extensive in Asia—is promoted by a military junta that seized power from an elected government in 1989. The country's officer corps is believed to be profiting handsomely from the receipts earned by selling these valuable hardwoods abroad. Unless the military's grip on power is loosened, millions of people whose futures are threatened by such practices will be powerless to stop them.[7]

Recently, there has been a heartening spread of democracy: In Eastern Europe, changes in Soviet foreign policy led to popular revolts, free elections, and independent governments. In Africa, democracies are beginning to emerge in Congo, Ethiopia, Ghana, Guinea,

Togo, Zaire, and Zambia. In Latin America, military dictatorships were swept aside from the Panamanian Isthmus to Tierra del Fuego. Brazil now has a democratically minded president and an ecologist as environment minister.

But authoritarian rule is still the norm in countries with more than one third of the world's people. And even where democracies exist in principle, a small elite often holds the reins of power, stifling dissent, arresting citizen activists, and sometimes rigging the electoral process. It is difficult to mount an environmental campaign in Malaysia, for example, when people can be arrested for marching as a group.[8]

The exercise of power is much rawer in developing than in rich nations. While U.S. corporations exert their muscle by financing political campaigns, chronic bribery and corruption provide more direct access in many countries. This leads to waste as well as the unsustainable use of resources. Zaire's problems, for instance, cannot be separated from the fact that its president reportedly amassed a fortune of $5 billion during his time in office—by systematically siphoning off funds earned by exporting the country's natural resources.[9]

One problem shared by many governments is wasteful spending on bloated military establishments. The U.N. Development Programme (UNDP) estimates that poor countries spent $146 billion on the military in 1989. Indeed, Third World military expenditures grew at the extraordinary rate of 7.5 percent annually from 1960 to 1987, while health, educational, and environmental programs were starved. Even with the demise of the cold war, old military conceptions of national security prevail in many nations. UNDP believes that by trimming unneeded military spending and cutting other wasteful programs, developing countries could free up $50 billion a year for real development.[10]

It is not only in developing countries that powerful economic interests feel threatened by the call for a new development path. In the United States, the oil, coal, and automobile industries strongly oppose policies to stabilize the climate by discouraging the use of fossil fuels. The power of such industries is based on their financial standing and the jobs they provide. But the hundreds of new industries and millions of jobs that could be created by energy policies to reduce greenhouse gases are not represented in the political process. The general public, which could benefit from the new climate policies, is not yet organized enough to push them through.[11]

In countries with democratic political systems, overcoming such barriers is a matter of political organizing, coalition building, and lobbying. Even in well-established democracies, however, some ingredients of full political participation are often not present. In much of Europe, the absence of right-to-know laws hinders citizen access to the information needed to promote environmental reforms. In the United States, the low rate of voting leaves many poor people unrepresented in legislatures. In Japan, the dearth of citizens' groups and the four-decade-long rule of the Liberal Democratic Party have kept the government insulated from the concerns of its people.

As national governments begin to take action, new measures of international leadership will likely be developed. Whereas in the past, global status has been measured by the size of a nation's military arsenal or the dollar value of its gross national product, neither of these is a good indicator of progress toward the more fundamental goal of a sustainable society. Increasingly, credit will go to countries such as Germany, which now stands alone among major countries in its plans to cut carbon dioxide emissions substantially. In a world in which "power" is measured in terms of sustainability, and national security is partly a matter of environmental health, a country with energy conservation, recycling, and foreign aid programs as strong as Denmark's or Switzerland's looks pretty good.

National government reforms are just the beginning of the institutional transformations needed to pursue a more sustainable path. The scientific community has the capacity to raise public understanding of environmental threats, as they have done so effectively on issues like ozone depletion. Educators have the ability to produce a generation of environmentally literate citizens, and the print and electronic media can spur the ongoing environmental education needed in an ever-changing world.

The business community also has a key role to play. Investment decisions will help determine whether an environmentally sustainable economic system emerges. Although corporations have traditionally fought against new pollution laws, many have adopted environmental goals and codes of responsibility in the past few years. McDonald's, for example, instituted a recycling program in 1991 that is intended to reduce waste 80 percent. Southern California Edison, an electric utility company, has moved ahead of its own national government by announcing plans to cut carbon dioxide emissions 20 percent by 2010.[12]

Another crucial plank in the campaign for a healthier planet is reform at the international level. With the emergence of global environmental issues—stratospheric ozone depletion, oceanic pollution, and the loss of plant and animal species—worldwide cooperation has become essential. Environmental concerns, more than any other, are a force binding the world's disparate societies into a global community.

Despite the enormity of the challenge, there is reason for optimism about the capacity for cooperation. As the nineties begin, the cold war that dominated international affairs for four decades and led to the militarization of the world economy is over. With its demise, the East-West conflict that guided foreign policies and shaped the world for more than a generation is being cast aside. The battle to save the planet could replace the battle over ideology as the organizing theme of international affairs. If we begin to fashion a promising future for the next generation, efforts to reverse the degradation of the planet will become increasingly prominent.[13]

For the first time since the emergence of the nation-state, all countries face the challenge of trying to unite around a common theme. The global agenda is likely to become as much ecological as ideological, dominated by the relationship between ourselves and nature. The cold war was largely an abstraction, a campaign waged by strategic planners. In the new struggle, people everywhere will be involved directly: consumers trying to recycle their garbage, couples trying to decide whether to have a second child, and peasants trying to conserve their topsoil. The goal of the cold war was to get others to change their values and behavior, but winning the battle to save the planet depends on changing our own.

The struggle for global environmental sustainability will not be conflict-free. The question of how to share responsibility for achieving a given goal, such as climate stabilization, could plague negotiations long after agree-

ment is reached on the goal itself. Indeed, as such deliberations proceed, sizable splits have already developed
between rich and poor countries. The political stresses
between East and West are likely to be replaced by the
economic and environmental stresses between North
and South, over such issues as the need to reduce Third
World debt, access to markets in the industrial North,
and allocation of the costs of environmental protection
between rich and poor.

Among the questions that emerge: Does responsible
global citizenship mean that those living in wealthy
countries have an obligation to reduce carbon dioxide
emissions to the level of those living in poor countries?
How should the cost of preserving the planet's diversity
of life be allocated among countries? Should repayment
of the "ecological debt" of wealthy countries—the environmental costs to the world of their industrialization—
be used to ease the financial debt of developing countries?

The struggle ahead was foreshadowed by the 1990
effort to agree on a rapid phaseout of chlorofluorocarbons (CFCs) to minimize further erosion of the stratospheric ozone layer. Faced with alarming new scientific
information, 93 countries agreed to halt CFC production in industrial countries by the end of this decade,
and in developing countries a decade later, going far
beyond the 1987 Montreal Protocol that called only for
a 50-percent cut. The agreement required extensive negotiation, in part because the scores of developing countries that so far have not contributed to ozone depletion
were reluctant to give up their right to produce CFCs at
some point in the future.[14]

The key debate came over the Third World's rights to
CFC substitutes developed by industrial-country corpo-

rations. European nations proposed a $240-million international fund to facilitate technology transfer, which brought support for the phaseout from developing countries, including India and China, the world's two most populous nations. However, the agreement was nearly scuttled by the United States, which has recently opposed additional multilateral funding of such initiatives. Only an eleventh-hour reversal by the U.S. government and a compromise on patent transfers saved the agreement.[15]

International diplomats face a full agenda of environmental treaties and agreements in the nineties. To be effective, they will need a solid grounding in ecology as well as politics and economics. At the global level, the Basel Convention on hazardous waste exports is still being ratified; the Law of the Sea treaty, originally negotiated in the seventies, continues to be implemented in bits and pieces; and the Antarctic Treaty regime has recently been reworked to establish a 50-year moratorium on mining and oil drilling.[16]

Early negotiations have also begun on two important and interrelated new treaties covering forestry and biodiversity. The idea is to protect some of the world's remaining natural areas, mostly located in the tropics, with technical and financial assistance to be provided by richer nations. Neither treaty is likely to be finally approved before the mid-nineties. Meanwhile, scores of regional treaties are in place or being considered that do everything from controlling transboundary air pollution in Europe to allocating the use of surface and groundwater resources between the United States and Mexico.[17]

Reaching agreement on a plan to stabilize climate is the ultimate challenge in environmental diplomacy. It is a problem that is global in scale and on which countries take divergent stances. Although industrial nations are the main contributors to the problem through their heavy use of fossil fuels, developing countries will also have to shift their development paths if the problem is ultimately to be resolved.

Diplomatic discussions on climate stabilization have been under way since early 1989, and diplomats hope to have a draft treaty ready by June 1992. An Intergovernmental Negotiating Committee was set up in Geneva in late 1990 under the auspices of the U.N. General Assembly, and formal governmental negotiating sessions are held every few months. Although most West European and several other industrial nations are already planning to limit carbon emissions, the United States— the largest offender—proposes to greatly increase its use of fossil fuels. While the Europeans have sought a strong treaty with specific commitments, the U.S. government continues to urge an agreement devoid of national targets or funding mechanisms.[18]

Developing countries are also divided on the question of how to deal with global warming. Although some small island nations are eager to see international commitments to slow climate change, China is planning to double its already heavy use of coal, a plan that would drive global greenhouse gas emissions upwards. Bridging such differences and providing developing countries with the technology and financing needed to pursue a new energy path will be crucial tests of the struggle for a new world order.[19]

Some 30 island countries, among the most obvious victims of rising sea level from a warming of the planet, have recently banded together to press for a strong climate treaty. Located mostly in the Indian Ocean, the Caribbean, and the South Pacific, these nations realize that their futures are shaped in part by the energy policies in larger industrial and developing economies. Leadership has come from the Republic of the Maldives, a collection of islands in the Indian Ocean where most of the land is barely two meters above the sea. Even a one-meter rise in sea level would, in the event of a storm surge, place the country's 140,000 residents in jeopardy.[20]

As countries search for new ways to address transnational threats, other ad hoc environmental alliances are likely to spring up. European countries could work together to save the region's deteriorating forests from acid rain, nations bordering the Baltic Sea could join to reverse its degradation, and countries in the Indian subcontinent could reforest the Himalayas. Such arrangements could one day become more numerous than the military alliances that have featured so prominently since World War II.

Another prime target for regional cooperation is in the management of water in the Middle East. The region draws upon three major river systems: the Tigris-Euphrates, the Jordan, and the Nile. Supplies are tight in the latter two, and tensions over water are high in all three regions. With the area's population growing at nearly 3 percent a year, water security is elusive. Cooperation in managing supplies and sharing water-saving technologies could stave off shortages, and buy time to slow population growth.[21]

The United Nations will have to assume a more prominent role if environmental threats are to be addressed on a more comprehensive basis. For one thing, if the UN were a more effective peacekeeper, as its founders envisaged, resources could be freed up for environmental purposes. Beyond its traditional roles, the

United Nations is at least trying to shoulder a growing responsibility for environmental protection efforts. The United Nations Environment Programme (UNEP), founded in 1972, helped facilitate the ozone accords, for example.[22]

The mammoth U.N. system, with its six governing bodies and 16 specialized agencies, is poorly equipped to deal with the challenge of environmentally sustainable development. The United Nations was founded in 1945, when environmental issues were hardly on the world agenda. Most U.N. agencies were formed in response to the problems of that era. There is, for instance, a large International Atomic Energy Agency, reporting directly to the General Assembly, but developing countries are given little help in obtaining the energy efficiency and renewable energy technologies that could benefit them. The Food and Agriculture Organization (FAO) is promoting unsustainable agricultural practices and also spearheading a Tropical Forestry Action Plan that in some cases may accelerate deforestation rather than arrest it.[23]

While environmental programs have been cobbled to the agendas of U.N. agencies, most are underfunded or staffed by people with little training. UNEP was intended to right this imbalance, but it never received the kind of clear mission, authority, or status that U.N. agencies enjoy. Its weak mandate stems in part from the international community's wariness in the early seventies about the proliferation of U.N. agencies. For two decades, UNEP has operated on voluntary contributions—recently its annual budget has totaled just $40 million, half that of some private U.S. environmental groups. UNEP is limited to trying to coordinate the environmental programs of its stronger brethren, taking on functions only when asked by governments to do so.[24]

The United Nations is only as strong as its member governments allow. The extraordinary political mobilization orchestrated through the U.N. Security Council in the months leading up to the 1991 Persian Gulf War was an example of what can be accomplished when governments are committed to a clear goal. Unfortunately, in the environmental arena, governments have been unwilling to provide sufficient funding or authority to U.N. bodies.

Yet the inability of governments to protect their citizens from global environmental threats has become frighteningly clear. National sovereignty has already been lost over such phenomena as ozone depletion and oceanic pollution. Just as communities depend on a police force to control the streets, so can national governments use international agencies to regain control over the global environment. Abraham Lincoln said that it is the role of governments to do for people what they cannot do for themselves. Likewise, it is the role of the United Nations to do for all people what national governments no longer can.[25]

The need for responsive U.N. environmental programs has become urgent: to collect important data, monitor treaty compliance, and provide financial support that allows the Third World to acquire the technology needed for a new development path. Moreover, environmentally sustainable development could be made part of the mandates of other agencies—particularly the U.N. Development Programme, which funds development projects, and FAO. It may also make sense to give a U.N. body the authority to order new initiatives when there is no time to wait for the negotiation of treaties. And it is crucial that international authorities be able to enforce such agreements. Accomplishing all of this and at the same time avoiding the inevitable tendency toward ineffectual, cumbersome international bureaucracies is a daunting task indeed.

Although national governments will remain the most powerful of human institutions for some time to come, their importance may already have peaked, as international institutions have taken on critical functions in recent years. Whether eliminating smallpox, fighting AIDS, or protecting the ozone layer, countries everywhere depend on the United Nations. The dependence is likely to grow as environmental monitoring and enforcement powers are vested in international agencies. Equally important are initiatives to decentralize power, in order to give local governments and grassroots organizations greater ability to develop solutions to their problems.

In recent years, citizens' environmental organizations have gone beyond their successful community projects to jointly lobby governments and petition international agencies. Although it is embarrassing for a government to have its request for a loan undermined by the complaints of an indigenous group, it is only by bridging the vast chasm between the grassroots and international diplomacy that the pace of change can be sufficiently accelerated. Amazonian rubber tappers at World Bank meetings and Penan tribal people in the corridors of the UN are important and encouraging signs of our times.[26]

The struggle for a sustainable world extends from the villages to the board rooms, from local town councils to the General Assembly in New York. Nowhere will it be easy, and at no point can its outcome be firmly predicted. This uncertainty provides the excitement of our age—and the challenge. In the end, we must ask how badly we want a sustainable future for our children. At the current pace of change, they are more likely to inherit a world of collapsing ecosystems, cancer epidemics, falling living standards, and recurrent famine.

We typically go to great lengths to provide for our children, investing heavily in education and health care. How much are we willing to invest in a habitable planet for them? At issue is whether we are collectively ready to make the effort, to undertake the struggle that is needed to bring a new world into being. As advertisers are fond of saying, this is a "limited time offer." It will soon expire.

Notes

CHAPTER 1. Uncover the Lifeboats!

1. Adapted from Bruce Wallace, "One Member's Views," submitted to the University Forum on Liberal Education, Virginia Polytechnic Institute and State University, Blacksburg, Va., June 1990.
2. World Environment Center, *The World Environment Handbook* (New York: 1985).
3. James Brooke, "Feeding on 19th Century Conditions, Cholera Spreads in Latin America," *New York Times*, April 21, 1991; Matt Moffett, "Best Things in Life Aren't Always Free in Mexico City," *Wall Street Journal*, May 8, 1991.
4. Jean-Paul Lanly, *Tropical Forest Resources* (Rome: U.N. Food and Agriculture Organization (FAO), 1982); H.E. Dregne, *Desertification of Arid Land* (New York: Harwood Academic Publishers, 1983); U.N. Environment Programme (UNEP), *General Assessment of Progress in the Implementation of the Plan of Action to Combat Desertification 1978–1984* (Nairobi: 1984); Lester R. Brown and Edward C. Wolf, *Soil Erosion: The Quiet Crisis in the World Econ-*

omy, Worldwatch Paper 60 (Washington, D.C.: Worldwatch Institute, September 1984); E.O. Wilson, ed., *Biodiversity* (Washington, D.C.: National Academy Press, 1988).

5. Kim Crews, Population Reference Bureau (PRB), personal communication, April 29, 1991; PRB, *1991 World Population Data Sheet* (Washington, D.C.: 1991); Angus Maddison, *The World Economy in the 20th Century* (Paris: Organisation for Economic Co-operation and Development (OECD), 1989); International Monetary Fund (IMF), *World Economic Outlook* (Washington, D.C.: October 1990).

6. Denis Hayes, "Earth Day 1990: Threshold of the Green Decade," *Natural History*, April 1990.

7. For a more detailed discussion of the differences between economists and ecologists, see the writings of Hazel Henderson, one of the pioneers in this field, especially *The Politics of the Solar Age: Alternatives to Economics* (Indianapolis, Ind.: Knowledge Systems, Inc., rev. ed., 1988).

8. Daniel Botkin, "Rethinking the Environment: A New Balance of Nature," *Wilson Quarterly*, Spring 1991.

9. Gross world economic output in 1990 from the 1988 gross world product from Central Intelligence Agency (CIA), *Handbook of Economic Statistics, 1989* (Washington, D.C.: 1989), with Soviet and Eastern Europe gross national products extrapolated from Paul Marer, *Dollar GNP's of the USSR and Eastern Europe* (Baltimore, Md.: Johns Hopkins University Press, 1985), with adjustments to 1990 based on growth rates from IMF, *World Economic Outlook*, and from CIA, *Handbook of Economic Statistics*, and with the composite deflator from Office of Management and Budget, *Historical Tables, Budget of the United States Government, Fiscal Year 1990* (Washington, D.C.: U.S. Government Printing Office, 1989); historical estimates based on Maddison, *The World Economy in the 20th Century*; international trade increase is Worldwatch Institute estimate based on IMF, *International Financial Statistics*, October 1990, and *Yearbook* (Washington, D.C.: 1990); U.S. Department of Commerce, "Standard and Poor Index of 500 Widely Held Stocks," Washington, D.C., 1990; Tokyo Stock Exchange, *Monthly Statistics Report*, June 1990.

10. Alan B. Durning, *Poverty and the Environment: Reversing the Downward Spiral*, Worldwatch Paper 92 (Washington, D.C.: November 1989); Robert S. McNamara, *The McNamara Years at the World Bank: Major Policy Addresses of Robert S. McNamara 1968–1981* (Baltimore, Md: Johns Hopkins University Press, 1981).

11. U.N. Children's Fund and UNEP, *Children and the Environment* (New York: 1990); "Beyond Perestroika: The Soviet Economy in Crisis," paper prepared by the CIA and the Defense Intelligence Agency for presentation to the Technology and National Security Subcommittee, Joint Economic Committee, U.S. Congress, Washington, D.C., May 14, 1991.

12. Neil Henry, "Worsening Famine Threatens 17 Million in 3 African Countries," *Washington Post*, May 24, 1991; International Labour Organization, *Economically Active Population Estimates, 1950–80, and Projections, 1985–2025*, Vol. 5 (Geneva: 1986); United Nations Development Programme, *Human Development Report 1991* (New York: Oxford University Press, 1991).

13. World Bank, *World Debt Tables 1990–1991: External Debt of Developing Countries Vol. I* (Washington, D.C.: 1990); U.N. Development Programme, *Human Development Report 1991* (New York: Oxford University Press, 1991).

14. FAO, "New Deforestation Rate Figures Announced," *Tropical Forest Programme* (IUCN Newsletter), August 1990; World Resources Institute, *World Resources, 1990–91* (New York: Oxford University Press, 1990); FAO, *Production Yearbook* (Rome: various years).

15. Dregne, *Desertification of Arid Land*.

16. "Vehicular Pollution Makes Breathing Dangerous," *Indian Post* (Bombay), February 11, 1989; Mark A. Uhlig, "Mexico City: the World's Foulest Air Grows Worse," *New York Times*, May 12, 1991; Mary Kay Magistad, "Bangkok's Progress Marked by Health Hazards," *Washington Post*, May 7, 1991.

17. "Sugar Maples Sicken Under Acid Rain's Pall," *New York Times*, May 15, 1991; British Petroleum, *BP Statistical Review of World Energy* (London: 1990); James N. Galloway et al., "Acid Rain: China, United States, and a Remote Area," *Science*, June 19, 1987.

18. W. Martin Williams et al., *Pesticides in Ground Water Data Base: 1988 Interim Report* (Washington, D.C.: Office of Pesticide Programs, U.S. Environmental Protection Agency (EPA), 1988); Stanley J. Kabala, "Poland: Facing the Hidden Costs of Development," *Environment*, November 1985; David E. Sanger, "Chemical Leak in Korea Brings Forth a New Era," *New York Times*, April 17, 1991.

19. N.F. Glazovsky, "The Aral Sea Crisis: The Source, the Current Situation, and the Ways to Solving It," presented to the international conference on the Aral Sea, Nukus, Soviet Karakalpak Republic, USSR, October 1–7, 1990; "Soviet Cotton Threatens

a Region's Sea—and its Children," *New Scientist*, November 18, 1989; USSR State Committee for the Protection of Nature, *Report on the State of the Environment in the USSR 1988* (Moscow: 1989); Murray Feshbach and Ann Rubin, "Why Ivan Can't Breathe," *Washington Post*, January 28, 1990.

20. William K. Reilly, "Statement on Ozone Depletion," EPA, Washington, D.C., April 4, 1991; "Ozone Loss Over U.S. Is Found To Be Twice as Bad as Predicted," *New York Times*, April 5, 1991.

21. Douglas G. Cogan, *Stones in a Glass House: CFCs and Ozone Depletion* (Washington, D.C.: Investor Responsibility Research Center, 1988).

22. Worldwatch Institute estimate based on Gregg Marland et al., *Estimates of CO_2 Emissions from Fossil Fuel Burning and Cement Manufacturing, Based on the United Nations Energy Statistics and the U.S. Bureau of Mines Cement Manufacturing Data* (Oak Ridge, Tenn.: Oak Ridge National Laboratory, 1989), on Gregg Marland, private communication and printout, Oak Ridge National Laboratory, Oak Ridge, Tenn., July 6, 1989, and on British Petroleum, *BP Statistical Review*; "Ministerial Declaration of the Second World Climate Conference," Second World Climate Conference, Geneva, November 7, 1990.

23. James E. Hansen, Goddard Institute for Space Studies, National Aeronautics and Space Administration, "The Green House Effect: Impacts on Current Global Temperature and Regional Heat Waves," Testimony before the Committee on Energy and Natural Resources, U.S. Senate, Washington, D.C., June 23, 1988; P.D. Jones, Climatic Research Unit, University of East Anglia, Norwich, U.K., "Testimony to the U.S. Senate on Global Temperatures," before the Commerce Committee, U.S. Senate, Washington, D.C., October 11, 1990; Richard A. Kerr, "Global Temperature Hits Record Again," *Science*, January 18, 1991.

24. Ariel E. Lugo, "Estimating Reductions in the Diversity of Tropical Forest Species," in Wilson, *Biodiversity*.

25. Herman E. Daly, "Sustainable Development: From Concept and Theory Towards Operational Principles," *Population and Development Review* (Proceedings of Hoover Institution Conference on Population and Development), forthcoming special issue.

CHAPTER 2. The Efficiency Revolution

1. "Final Conference Statement: Scientific/Technical Sessions," Second World Climate Conference, Geneva, November 7, 1990.
2. Ibid.; U.S. Environmental Protection Agency, *Policy Options for Stabilizing Global Climate* (Washington, D.C.: 1990).
3. "Emission Targets and Timetables: Other OECD Countries," prepared for the Twentieth Annual ABA conference on the Environment, Warrenton, Va., May 18, 1991; "The Carbon Club," *Atmosphere*, June 1991; "Ministerial Declaration of the Second World Climate Conference," Second World Climate Conference, Geneva, November 7, 1990.
4. Roger S. Carlsmith et al., "Energy Efficiency: How Far Can We Go?" Oak Ridge National Laboratory, Oak Ridge, Tenn., prepared for the Office of Policy, Planning and Analysis, U.S. Department of Energy (DOE), in support of the National Energy Strategy, January 1990; Birgit Bodlund et al., "The Challenge of Choices: Technology Options for the Swedish Electricity Sector," in T.B. Johansson et al., *Electricity: Efficient End-Use and New Generation Technologies, and Their Planning Implications* (Lund, Sweden: Lund University Press, 1989); William U. Chandler, ed., *Carbon Emissions Control Strategies: Case Studies in International Cooperation* (Washington, D.C.: World Wildlife Fund and The Conservation Foundation, 1990); "Canadian Energy Ministers Fail to Agree on Reduction in Carbon Dioxide," *International Environment Reporter*, September 13, 1989; Commission of the European Communities, Directorate-General for Energy, "Energy for a New Century: The European Perspective," *Energy in Europe*, special issue, July 1990.
5. Christopher Flavin and Alan Durning, *Building on Success: The Age of Energy Efficiency*, Worldwatch Paper 82 (Washington, D.C.: Worldwatch Institute, March 1988).
6. Ibid.; Arthur Rosenfeld and David Hafemeister, "Energy-Efficient Building," *Scientific American*, April 1988; Peter Weiss, "Lighting the Way Towards More Efficient Lighting," *Home Energy*, January/February 1989.
7. Ashok Gadgil et al., "Advanced Lighting and Window Technologies for Reducing Electricity Consumption and Peak Demand: Overseas Manufacturing and Marketing Opportunities," Lawrence Berkeley Laboratory, Berkeley, Calif., March 1991; Edwin A. Moore and George Smith, "Capital Expenditures for Electric Power in Developing Countries in the 1990s," Energy Series Paper No. 21 , World Bank, Washington, D.C., February 1990.

8. José Goldemberg et al., "An End-Use Oriented Global Energy Strategy," in Annual Review, Inc., *Annual Review of Energy*, Vol. 10 (Palo Alto, Calif.: 1985); "Third World Home Designed to Show 'Small is Beautiful,' " *Journal of Commerce*, May 28, 1991.

9. Jorgen Norgaard, Technical University of Denmark, Lyngby, Denmark, private communications, October 28–29, 1987; Howard Geller, "Energy-Efficient Residential Appliances: Performance Issues and Policy Options," *IEEE Technology and Society Magazine*, March 1986; David B. Goldstein and Peter Miller, "Developing Cost Curves for Conserved Energy in New Refrigerators and Freezers," American Council for an Energy-Efficient Economy, Washington, D.C., 1986.

10. Marc Ross, "Industrial Energy Conservation," *National Resource Journal*, August 1984; Marc Ross, "Industrial Energy Conservation and the Steel Industry," *Energy, The International Journal*, October/November 1987.

11. U.S. Congress, Office of Technology Assessment (OTA), *Industrial Energy Use* (Washington, D.C.: U.S. Government Printing Office, 1983); Tina Brohmann, regional planner, OKO Institute, Darmstadt, Germany, private communication, July 12, 1991.

12. Table 2–1 is from Worldwatch Institute based on Mary C. Holcomb et al., *Transportation Energy Data Book: Edition 9* (Oak Ridge, Tenn.: Oak Ridge National Laboratory, 1987), on Vuvan R. Vuchic, *Urban Public Transportation Systems and Technology* (Englewood Cliffs, N.J.: Prentice-Hall, 1981), on Deborah Bleviss, *The New Oil Crisis and Fuel Economy Technologies: Preparing the Light Transportation Industry for the 1990's* (New York: Quorum Press, 1988), on Marcia D. Lowe, *Alternatives to the Automobile: Transport for Livable Cities*, Worldwatch Paper 98 (Washington, D.C.: Worldwatch Institute, October 1990), and on David Woodruff and Thane Peterson, "The Greening of Detroit," *Business Week*, April 8, 1991; solar electric car from Anita Rajan, Solectria Corporation, Arlington, Mass., private communication, April 17, 1991.

13. "Fresh Charge of the Electric Brigade," *Financial Times*, April 11, 1991; Woodruff and Peterson, "The Greening of Detroit."

14. Lowe, *Alternatives to the Automobile*.

15. Susan E. Owens, "Land Use Planning for Energy Efficiency," in J. Barry Cullingworth, ed., *Energy, Land and Public Policy* (New Brunswick, N.J.: Transaction Publishers, 1990).

16. Ibid.

17. Bundesministerium für Verkehr, *Verkehr in Zahlen 1987* (Bonn:

1987); Peter Newman and Jeffrey Kenworthy, *Cities and Automobile Dependence: An International Sourcebook* (Aldershot, U.K.: Gower, 1989); Lowe, *Alternatives to the Automobile*.

18. Marcia D. Lowe, *The Bicycle: Vehicle for a Small Planet*, Worldwatch Paper 90 (Washington, D.C.: Worldwatch Institute, September 1989); A. Wilmink, "The Effects of State Subsidizing of Bicycle Facilities," *Velo City '87 Congress: Planning for the Urban Cyclist*, proceedings of the Third International Velo City Congress, Groningen, the Netherlands, September 22–26, 1987; Michael A. Replogle, "Major Bikeway Construction Effort in the Netherlands," *Urban Transportation Abroad*, Winter 1982; David Peltz, Davis Department of Public Works, Davis, Calif., private communication, July 28, 1989; Michael A. Replogle, *Bicycles and Public Transportation: New Links to Suburban Transit Markets*, 2nd ed. (Washington, D.C.: The Bicycle Federation, 1988).

19. Fred Sissine, Congressional Research Service, "Telecommuting: A National Option for Conserving Oil," Testimony before the Subcommittee on Water, Power and Offshore Energy Resources, U.S. House of Representatives, September 11, 1990.

20. Ashok B. Boghani et al., "Can Telecommunications Help Solve America's Transportation Problems?" Arthur D. Little, Cambridge, Mass., 1991.

21. Owens, "Land Use Planning for Energy Efficiency"; Michael B. Brough, "Density and Dimensional Regulations, Article XII," *A Unified Development Ordinance* (Washington, D.C.: American Planning Association, Planners Press, 1985); "Country Profiles: Denmark," *European Energy Report*, May 1990.

22. Mark D. Levine et al., "Energy Efficiency, Developing Nations, and Eastern Europe," A Report to the U.S. Working Group on Global Energy Efficiency, April 1991.

23. U.S. Congress, OTA, *Energy in Developing Countries* (Washington, D.C.: 1991); Levine et al., "Energy Efficiency, Developing Nations, and Eastern Europe."

24. Amulya K.N. Reddy, "Energy Strategies for a Sustainable Development in India," presented at conference on Global Collaboration on a Sustainable Energy Development, Copenhagen, April 25–28, 1991.

25. U.S. Bureau of the Census, *Statistical Abstract of the United States: 1990* (Washington, D.C.: U.S. Government Printing Office, 1990); DOE, Energy Information Administration, *Monthly Energy Review, February 1990* (Washington, D.C.: May 1990); Edison Electric Institute, *Statistical Yearbook of the Electric Utility Industry/1988* (Washington, D.C.: 1989).

26. International Labour Organization, *Yearbook of Labour Statistics 1988* (Geneva: 1988); "Germany to End Coal Subsidy?" *Business Europe*, London, April 6, 1990; William Chandler, Pacific Northwest Laboratories, Washington, D.C., private communication, July 26, 1990; "Reduced Use of Brown Coal and Its Products Called Top East German Environmental Goals," *International Environment Reporter*, March 18, 1990; World Bank, *China: Socialist Economic Development*, Volume II (Washington, D.C.: 1983); World Bank, *China: The Energy Sector* (Washington, D.C.: 1985).

27. Steven Buchsbaum and James W. Benson, *Jobs and Energy: The Employment and Economic Impacts of Nuclear Power, Conservation, and Other Energy Options* (New York: Council on Economic Priorities, 1979).

28. Olav Hohmeyer et al., *Employment Effects of Energy Conservation Investments in EC Countries* (Luxembourg: Office for Official Publications of the European Communities, 1985); Steve Colt, University of Alaska–Anchorage, "Income and Employment Impacts of Alaska's Low Income Weatherization Program," ISER Working Paper 89.2, Prepared for Second Annual Rural Energy Conference, Anchorage, Alaska, October 12, 1989; Meridian Corporation, *Iowa Weatherization Assistance Program Evaluation* (Alexandria, Va.: 1988); State of Connecticut, Office of Policy and Management, Energy Division, *An Initial Analysis of Low Income Weatherization Issues in Connecticut* (Hartford, Conn.: Office of Policy and Management, Energy Division, 1988).

29. Michelle Yesney, "Sustainable City Project Annual Report and Recommendation," City of San Jose, Calif., Memorandum, February 22, 1990; Skip Laitner, "Fiscal and Economic Analysis of the Proposed 1990 Energy Management Program for San Jose," prepared for the city of San Jose, Calif., Economic Research Associates, Eugene, Oreg., January 30, 1990.

CHAPTER 3. Building a Solar Economy

1. "Nuclear Power Reactors in the World," International Atomic Energy Agency, Vienna, April 1991; "East German Nuclear Plant Hopes Fade as Minister Changes Tack," *European Energy Report*, April 19, 1991; Charles Mitchell, "Fallout from Chernobyl Accident Still Clouds Soviet Nuclear Plans," *Journal of Commerce*, April 19, 1991.

2. John J. Taylor, "Improved and Safer Nuclear Power," *Science*, April 21, 1989; "Outlook on Advanced Reactors," *Nucleonics*

Week, March 20, 1989; R.H. Williams and H.A. Feiveson, "Diversion-Resistance Criteria for Future Nuclear Power," Center for Energy and Environmental Studies, Princeton University, Princeton, N.J., May 22, 1989; Klaus Michael Meyerabich and Bertram Schefold, *Die Grenzen der Atomwitschaft* (Munich: Verlag C.H. Beck, 1986).

3. Accessible resources are that portion of the "total resource base that can be exploited with currently available technology or technology that will soon be available," from Meridian Corporation, "Characterization of U.S. Energy Resources and Reserves," prepared for Deputy Assistant Secretary for Renewable Energy, Department of Energy (DOE), Alexandria, Va., June 1989; Idaho National Engineering Laboratory (INEL) et al., *The Potential of Renewable Energy: An Interlaboratory White Paper*, prepared for the Office of Policy, Planning and Analysis, DOE, in support of the National Energy Strategy (Golden, Colo.: Solar Energy Research Institute (SERI), 1990); DOE, Energy Information Administration (EIA), *Annual Energy Review 1989* (Washington, D.C.: 1990).

4. J.M.O. Scurlock and D.O. Hall, "The Contribution of Biomass to Global Energy Use," *Biomass*, No. 21, 1990; Norwegian figure is based on Norwegian Central Bureau of Statistics, *Natural Resources and the Environment, 1989* (Oslo: 1990), wherein more than 45 percent of total supply is from hydroelectric power and 5 percent from biomass.

5. Carl J. Weinberg and Robert H. Williams, "Energy from the Sun," *Scientific American*, September 1990; Table 3–1 based on INEL et al., *The Potential of Renewable Energy*, on Christopher Flavin and Rick Piltz, *Sustainable Energy* (Washington, D.C.: Renew America, 1989), on DOE, *Energy Technologies & the Environment* (Washington, D.C.: 1988), on Peggy Sheldon, Luz International Limited, Los Angeles, Calif., private communication and printout, August 28, 1990, on Susan Williams and Kevin Porter, *Power Plays* (Washington, D.C.: Investor Responsibility Research Center, 1989), and on Nancy Rader et al., *Power Surge* (Washington, D.C.: Public Citizen, 1989); "Country Profiles: Denmark," *European Energy Report*, May 1990; "Spain Resurrects Funding Programme," *European Energy Report*, July 13, 1990; "West Germany Announces $3bn Plan for Research and Technology," *European Energy Report*, March 9, 1990.

6. Low-temperature heat is Worldwatch Institute estimate, based on Amory B. Lovins, *Soft Energy Paths: Toward a Durable Peace* (Cambridge, Mass.: Ballinger Publishing Company, 1977), on John Hebo Nielsen, "Denmark's Energy Future," *Energy Policy*,

January/February 1990, and on DOE, EIA, *Annual Energy Review 1989*; Solar Technical Information Program, *Energy for Today: Renewable Energy* (Golden, Colo.: SERI, 1990).

7. Rick Bevington and Arthur H. Rosenfeld, "Energy for Buildings and Homes," *Scientific American*, September 1990; Joyce Whitman, *The Environment in Israel* (Jerusalem: Environmental Protection Service, Ministry of the Interior, 1988); Mark Newham, "Jordan's Solution Circles the Sky," *Energy Economist*, June 1989; Eric Young, "Aussies to Test Novel Solar Energy Collector," *Energy Daily*, May 3, 1990; Solar Technical Information Program, *Energy for Today: Renewable Energy*; Nicholas P. Lenssen, "Cooked by the Sun," *World Watch*, March/April 1989.

8. Sheldon, private communication and printout; Don Logan, Luz International Limited, Los Angeles, Calif., private communication, September 26, 1990; Bureau of the Census, U.S. Department of Commerce, *Statistical Abstract of the United States 1990* (Washington, D.C.: U.S. Government Printing Office, 1990).

9. INEL et al., *The Potential of Renewable Energy*.

10. Figure 3–1 from Cynthia Pollock Shea, *Renewable Energy: Today's Contribution, Tomorrow's Promise*, Worldwatch Paper 81 (Washington, D.C.: Worldwatch Institute, January 1988), with 1987–90 data from "Production of PV Modules Worldwide Rises 14% To Record 48 MW During 1990," *Photovoltaic Insider's Report*, February 1991; Steven Dickman, "The Sunny Side of the Street. . .," *Nature*, May 3, 1990; "Sanyo Develops Solar Cell Shingles," *Independent Energy*, April 1989.

11. DOE, *Energy Technologies & the Environment*; DOE, *Photovoltaic Energy Program Summary* (Washington, D.C.: 1990); Ken Zweibel, *Harnessing Solar Power: The Photovoltaics Challenge* (New York: Plenum Publishing, 1990); Meridian Corporation and IT Power Limited, "Learning from Success: Photovoltaic-Power Water Pumping in Mali," prepared for U.S. Committee on Renewable Energy Commerce and Trade, Alexandria, Va., February 20, 1990; Maheshwar Dayal, Secretary, Department of Non-Conventional Energy Sources, New Delhi, India, private communication, July 13, 1989; "Indonesia Installs First Solar Village, Schedules Total of 2,000," *International Solar Energy Intelligence Report*, February 9, 1990; "A New Group of Sun Worshippers," *Asiaweek*, October 12, 1990.

12. Zweibel, *Harnessing Solar Power*; INEL et al., *The Potential of Renewable Energy*.

13. Flavin and Piltz, *Sustainable Energy*; INEL et al., *The Potential of Renewable Energy*; Danish experience from Paul Gipe, "Wind

Energy Comes of Age," Gipe & Assoc., Tehachapi, Calif., May 13, 1990.

14. U.S. Windpower, Inc., "The Design Specifications for a Wind Power Plant in Patagonia Using U.S. Wind Turbines," Livermore, Calif., January 1989; Christopher Flavin, *Wind Power: A Turning Point*, Worldwatch Paper 45 (Washington, D.C.: Worldwatch Institute, July 1981); "Minnesota Resource Greater than Previously Reported," *Wind Energy Weekly* (American Wind Energy Association, Washington, D.C.), July 5, 1990.

15. P.J. de Groot and D.O. Hall, "Biomass Energy: A New Perspective," prepared for the African Energy Policy Research Network, University of Botswana, Gaborone, January 8, 1990; P.P.S. Gusain, *Cooking Energy in India* (Delhi: Vikas Publishing House, 1990).

16. Lester R. Brown, *The Changing World Food Prospect: The Nineties and Beyond*, Worldwatch Paper 85 (Washington, D.C.: Worldwatch Institute, October 1988); Sandra Postel, *Water for Agriculture: Facing the Limits*, Worldwatch Paper 93 (Washington, D.C.: Worldwatch Institute, December 1989); Biofuels and Municipal Waste Technology Program, Office of Renewable Energy Technologies, DOE, *Five Year Research Plan: 1988–1992, Biofuels: Renewable Fuels for the Future* (Springfield, Va.: National Technical Information Service, 1988); Norman Hinman, SERI, Golden, Colo., private communication, August 25, 1989.

17. Charles G. Gunnerson and David C. Stuckey, "Anaerobic Digestion: Principles and Practices for Biogas Systems," World Bank Technical Paper No. 49, 1986; Eric D. Larson et al., "Biomass Gasification for Gas Turbine Power Generation," in T.B. Johansson et al., *Electricity: Efficient End-Use and New Generation Technologies, and Their Planning Implications* (Lund, Sweden: Lund University Press, 1989); Eric D. Larson et al., "Biomass-Gasifier Steam-Injected Gas Turbine Cogeneration for the Cane Sugar Industry," presented at the Energy from Biomass and Wastes XIV conference, Lake Buena Vista, Fla., January 29-February 2, 1990; United Nations, *1988 Energy Statistics Yearbook* (New York: 1990).

18. United Nations, *1988 Energy Statistics Yearbook*; Satyajit K. Singh, "Evaluating Large Dams in India," *Economic and Political Weekly*, March 17, 1990.

19. Donald Finn, Geothermal Energy Institute, New York, private communication and printout, March 16, 1990; United Nations, *1988 Energy Statistics Yearbook*; Phillip Michael Wright, "Devel-

opments in Geothermal Resources, 1983–1988," *The American Association of Petroleum Geologist Bulletin*, October 1989; New Energy Development Organization, "The Map of Prospective Geothermal Fields in Japan," Tokyo, 1984, as cited in Michael J. Grubb, "The Cinderella Options: A Study of Modernized Renewable Energy Technologies, Part 2: Political and Policy Analysis," *Energy Policy*, October 1990.

20. Joan Ogden and Robert Williams, *Solar Hydrogen* (Washington, D.C.: World Resources Institute, 1989); Robert Wills, "Hydrogen Fuel Cells: The Power Source of the 90's," *Northeast Sun*, Summer 1991.

21. British Petroleum, Ltd., *BP Statistical Review of World Energy* (London: 1990).

22. Amory B. Lovins, "Energy Strategy: The Road Not Taken?" *Foreign Affairs*, October 1976; INEL et al., *The Potential of Renewable Energy*; Carl J. Weinberg and Robert H. Williams, "Energy from the Sun," *Scientific American*, September 1990.

23. Christopher Flavin and Nicholas Lenssen, *Beyond the Petroleum Age: Designing a Solar Economy*, Worldwatch Paper 100 (Washington, D.C.: Worldwatch Institute, December 1990).

24. Table 3–2 is from Worldwatch Institute, based on Meridian Corporation, "Energy System Emissions and Material Requirements," prepared for DOE, Alexandria, Va., February 1989, on Paul Savoldelli, Luz International Limited, Los Angeles, Calif., private communication and printout, July 11, 1989, on Paula Blaydes, California Energy Company, San Francisco, Calif., private communication, June 19, 1990, and on Gipe, "Wind Energy Comes of Age."

25. The photovoltaic panels would actually cover just 15 percent of this land area; John Schaefer and Edgar DeMeo, Electric Power Research Institute, "An Update on U.S. Experiences with Photovoltaic Power Generation," Proceedings of the American Power Conference, April 23, 1990; U.S. land area used by the military from Michael Renner, "Assessing the Military's War on the Environment," in Lester R. Brown et al., *State of the World 1991* (New York: W.W. Norton, 1991), based on U.S. Department of Defense, *Our Nation's Defense and the Environment. A Department of Defense Initiative* (Washington, D.C.: 1990), on Michael Satchell, "Operation Land-Grab," *U.S. News and World Report*, May 14, 1990, on Edward McGlinn, "The Military Land Grab," *The Riverwatch*, Anglers of the Au Sable River, Grayling, Mich., Winter 1990, and on Thomas B. Cochran et al., *Nuclear Weapons Databook, Vol. II: U.S. Nuclear Warhead Production* (Cambridge, Mass.: Ballinger, 1987); Randall

Swisher, Executive Director, American Wind Energy Association, Washington, D.C., press release, September 25, 1990, based on D.L. Elliott et al., Pacific Northwest Laboratories, Richland, Wash., "U.S. Areal Wind Resource Estimates Considering Environmental and Land-Use Exclusions," presented at the American Wind Energy Association Windpower '90 Conference, Washington, D.C., September 28, 1990.

26. J. Davidson, "Bioenergy Tree Plantations in the Tropics: Ecological Implications and Impacts," Commission on Ecology Paper No. 12, International Union for Conservation of Nature and Natural Resources, Gland, Switzerland, 1987; Zweibel, *Harnessing Solar Power*; ethanol and electric car comparison is a Worldwatch Institute estimate, based on Jim MacKenzie, "Powering Transportation in the Future: Methanol from Trees or Electricity from Solar Cells?" World Resources Institute, Washington, D.C., March 26, 1987, on U.S. Environmental Protection Agency, Office of Mobile Sources, *Analysis of the Economic and Environmental Effects of Ethanol as an Automotive Fuel* (Ann Arbor, Mich.: April, 1990), and on Savoldelli, private communication and printout; William Babbitt, Associated Appraisers, Cheyenne, Wyo., private communication, October 11, 1990; U.S. Department of Agriculture, Economic Research Service, *Agricultural Resources: Agricultural Land Values and Markets Situation and Outlook Report*, Washington, D.C., June 1990; Gipe, "Wind Energy Comes of Age."

27. Table 3–3 is from Worldwatch Institute based on DOE, EIA, *Electric Plant Cost and Power Production Expenses 1988* (Washington, D.C.: 1990), on DOE, EIA, *Coal Production Statistics 1988* (Washington, D.C.: 1989), on Mark Sisinyak, Vice President, California Energy Company, Coso Junction, Calif., private communication, June 19, 1990, on Kathleen Flanagan, Director of Government Relations and Public Affairs, Luz International Limited, Los Angeles, Calif., private communication, June 18, 1990, and on Paul Gipe, Gipe & Assoc., Tehachapi, Calif., private communication, April 12, 1990; Neill and Gunter Limited, "A Study of the Socio-Economic Impact of Wood Energy 1988–2008 in New Brunswick," prepared for the New Brunswick Department of Natural Resources and Energy, Fredericton, N.B., Canada, October 1989.

28. International Energy Agency (IEA), *Energy Policies and Programmes of IEA Countries, 1989 Review* (Paris: Organisation for Economic Co-operation and Development, 1990); "World Status Report; Fusion Power," *Energy Economist*, June 1988.

CHAPTER 4. Reusing and Recycling Materials

1. Share of various discarded materials and energy savings of aluminum and glass recycling from Cynthia Pollock, *Mining Urban Wastes: The Potential for Recycling*, Worldwatch Paper 76 (Washington, D.C.: Worldwatch Institute, April 1987); energy savings of steel recycling from William U. Chandler, *Materials Recycling: The Virtue of Necessity*, Worldwatch Paper 56 (Washington, D.C.: Worldwatch Institute, October 1983); energy savings of newsprint recycling from Roberta Forsell Stauffer, "Energy Savings From Recycling," *Resource Recycling*, January/February 1989.

2. L.L. Gaines, *Energy and Materials Use in the Production and Recycling of Consumer-Goods Packaging* (Argonne, Ill.: Argonne National Laboratory, 1981).

3. Pollock, *Mining Urban Wastes*.

4. U.S. Environmental Protection Agency (EPA), Office of Solid Waste and Emergency Response (OSWER), *Report to Congress: Wastes from the Extraction and Benefication of Metallic Ores, Phosphate Rock, Asbestos, Overburden from Uranium Mining, and Oil Shale* (Washington, D.C.: U.S. Government Printing Office, 1985); municipal solid waste from EPA, OSWER, *Characterization of Municipal Solid Waste in the United States: 1990 Update* (Washington, D.C.: 1990); for an extended discussion of the issue at the international level, see John E. Young, *Discarding the Throwaway Society*, Worldwatch Paper 101 (Washington, D.C.: January 1991).

5. U.S. Department of State, Council on Environmental Quality, *The Global 2000 Report to the President: Entering the Twenty-First Century* (New York: Penguin Books, 1982).

6. Chandler, *Materials Recycling*; Pollock, *Mining Urban Wastes*.

7. Donald F. Barnett and Robert W. Crandall, *Up From the Ashes: The Rise of the Steel Minimill in the United States* (Washington, D.C.: Brookings Institution, 1986).

8. Krystal Miller, "On the Road Again and Again and Again: Auto Makers Try to Build Recyclable Car," *Wall Street Journal*, April 30, 1991; "Old Cars Get a New Lease of Life," (London) *Financial Times*, April 3, 1991; Bill Siuru, "Car Recycling in Germany," *Resource Recycling*, February 1991.

9. Cynthia Pollock Shea, "Disarming Refrigerators," *World Watch*, May/June 1991.

10. Ibid.

11. Tellus Institute, *CSG/Tellus Packaging Study: Literature and Pub-*

lic Policy Review (Boston: 1990); Laurids Mikaelsen, Economic Minister, Embassy of Denmark, Washington, D.C., private communication, May 3, 1991.

12. Kirsten U. Oldenburg and Joel S. Hirschhorn, "Waste Reduction: A New Strategy to Avoid Pollution," *Environment*, March 1987.

13. Barbara Baklarz, Amercian Telephone & Telegraph (AT&T), Basking Ridge, N.J., private communication, May 23, 1991; AT&T, "A Clean and Healthy Planet: AT&T Environment & Safety Report on Activies 1990," public relations document.

14. "Cost of Packaging Food Could Exceed Farm Net," *Journal of Commerce*, August 12, 1986.

15. Table 4–1 based on Gaines, *Energy and Materials Use*; Ontario example from John Miles, Tomra Systems Inc., London, Ont., Canada, private communication to Pat Franklin, National Container Recycling Coalition, Washington, D.C., October 23, 1990.

16. Lester R. Brown and Jodi L. Jacobson, *The Future of Urbanization: Facing the Ecological and Economic Constraints*, Worldwatch Paper 77 (Washington, D.C.: Worldwatch Institute, May 1987); Shanghai example from Yue-Man Yeung, "Urban Agriculture in Asia," The Food Energy Nexus Program of the United Nations University, Tokyo, September 1985.

17. Peter Edwards, *Aquaculture: A Component of Low Cost Sanitation Technology* (Washington, D.C.: U.N. Development Programme and World Bank, 1985).

18. Carl Woestendiek, Seattle Solid Waste Utility, Seattle, Wash., private communication, August 8, 1990.

CHAPTER 5. Protecting the Biological Base

1. Peter M. Vitousek et al., "Human Appropriation of the Products of Photosynthesis," *BioScience*, June 1986.

2. Sandra Postel and Lori Heise, *Reforesting the Earth*, Worldwatch Paper 83 (Washington, D.C.: Worldwatch Institute, April 1988); U.N. Food and Agriculture Organization (FAO), which is in the midst of preparing a new global forest assessment, according to "New Deforestation Rate Figures Announced," *Tropical Forest Programme* (IUCN Newsletter), August 1990.

3. Edward C. Wolf, "Survival of the Rarest," *World Watch*, March/April 1991.

4. Walter V.C. Reid, "Sustainable Development: Lessons from Success," *Environment*, May 1989; Charles M. Peters et al., "Valuation of an Amazonian Rainforest," *Nature*, June 29, 1989.

5. Duncan Poore, *No Timber Without Trees: Sustainability in the Tropical Forest* (London: Earthscan Publications Ltd, 1989); Peter H. Morrison, *Old Growth in the Pacific Northwest: A Status Report* (Washington, D.C.: The Wilderness Society, 1988).

6. John C. Ryan, "Oregon's Ancient Laboratory," *World Watch*, November/December 1990; Gary S. Hartshorn et al., "Sustained Yield Management of Tropical Forests: A Synopsis of the Palcazu Development Project in the Central Selva of the Peruvian Amazon," in J.C. Figueroa C. et al., eds., *Management of the Forests of Tropical America: Prospects and Technologies* (Rio Piedras, P.R.: Institute of Tropical Forestry, 1987).

7. Sandra Postel and John C. Ryan, "Reforming Forestry," in Lester R. Brown et al., *State of the World 1991* (New York: W.W. Norton & Co., 1991).

8. Lester R. Brown et al., "Outlining a Global Action Plan," in Lester R. Brown et al., *State of the World 1989* (New York: W.W. Norton & Co., 1989).

9. FAO, *Production Yearbook* (Rome: 1989).

10. Based on estimate for Asia and Africa from James Yazman, Program Officer in Animal Sciences, Winrock International, Morrilton, Ark., private communication, May 30, 1991.

11. From Harold E. Dregne, according to Till Darnhofer, U.N. Environment Programme, Nairobi, Kenya, private communication, May 23, 1991; FAO, *Production Yearbook*.

12. Mark Poffenberger, "Joint Management for Forest Lands: Experiences from South Asia," Ford Foundation, New Delhi, India, January 1990.

13. FAO, *Fishery Statistics Yearbook* (Rome: 1989); FAO, *Production Yearbook*; Clarence Idyll and Virgil Norton, *Recommended Actions for the United States Agency for International Development in Support of Fisheries Development* (report prepared by Chemonics International Consulting Division), Geneva, February 1988.

14. FAO, "Review of the State of World Fishery Resources," Rome, July 1983.

15. Jim Ketcham-Colwill, "Acid Rain: Science and Control Issues," Environmental and Energy Study Institute Special Report, July 12, 1989; U.N. Economic Commission for Europe, "Current Geographical Extent of Acidification in Rivers, Lakes, and Reservoirs in the ECE Region" (draft), Washington, D.C., June 15, 1988; Bostwick H. Ketchum, ed., *Ecosystems of the World, Vol. 26, Estuaries and Enclosed Seas* (Amsterdam: Elsevier Scientific Publishing Co., 1983).

16. Phillip P. Micklin, "The Water Management Crisis in Soviet Central Asia," final report to the National Council for Soviet

and East European Research, Washington, D.C., February 1989; Phillip P. Micklin, "Desiccation of the Aral Sea: A Water Management Disaster in the Soviet Union," *Science*, September 2, 1988.

17. U.S. Department of Commerce, Bureau of the Census, *Statistical Abstract of the United States 1990* (Washington, D.C.: 1990).

18. FAO, "Aquaculture Production (1984–1987)," Fisheries Circular No. 815, Revision 1, Rome, November 1989; Raymond J. Rhodes, "Status of World Aquaculture: 1987," *Aquaculture Magazine Buyer's Guide*, 1988.

19. Sandra Postel, "Halting Land Degradation," in Brown et al., *State of the World 1989*.

20. Zimbabwe example from "Families' Value," *The Economist*, January 26, 1991.

CHAPTER 6. Grain for Eight Billion

1. Authors' calculations based on data from the U.S. Department of Agriculture (USDA); World Bank, *World Development Report 1990* (New York: Oxford University Press, 1990); U.N. Department of International Economic and Social Affairs, *World Population Prospects 1988* (New York: 1989); authors' estimate based on USDA data.

2. USDA, Economic Research Service (ERS), *World Grain Database* (unpublished printouts) (Washington, D.C.: 1990).

3. Ibid.; Harold E. Dregne, *Desertification of Arid Land* (New York: Harwood Academic Publishers, 1983); Lester R. Brown, *The Worldwide Loss of Cropland*, Worldwatch Paper 24 (Washington, D.C.: Worldwatch Institute, October 1978).

4. Gu Chengwen, "Industries Eating Up the Nation's Best Land," *China Daily*, March 11, 1989; P.T. Bangsberg, "China Safeguards Agricultural Areas," *Journal of Commerce*, October 24, 1988.

5. USDA, ERS, *China Agriculture and Trade Report*, Washington, D.C., July 1990; Sophia Huang, USDA, ERS, private communication, May 24, 1991.

6. Visit by Sandra Postel to North China Plain, June 1988.

7. Holly B. Brough, "A New Lay of the Land," *World Watch*, January/February 1991.

8. U.N. Food and Agriculture Organization (FAO), *Production Yearbook* (Rome: various years).

9. Ibid.

10. Frits van der Leeden et al., *The Water Encyclopedia* (Chelsea, Mich.: Lewis Publishers, Inc., 1990); Sandra Postel, *Conserving*

Water: The Untapped Alternative, Worldwatch Paper 67 (Washington, D.C.: Worldwatch Institute, September 1985); Henry Kamm, "Israel's Farming Success Drains It of Water," *New York Times*, April 21, 1991.

11. FAO, *Production Yearbook*.

12. FAO, *Fertilizer Yearbook* (Rome: various years); The Fertilizer Institute, *1991 Fertilizer Facts and Figures* (Washington, D.C.: 1991); K. F. Isherwood and K. G. Soh, "The Medium Term Supply and Demand Prospects for Fertilizer Materials, Part I–The Agricultural Situation and Fertilizer Demand," International Fertilizer Industry Association Annual Conference, London, May 1991, updated June 1991.

13. Based on FAO, *Fertilizer Yearbook* (Rome: 1988), and on FAO, *Production Yearbook*.

14. FAO, *Fertilizer Yearbook* (various years); FAO, *Production Yearbook*.

15. Robert J.L. Hawke, Prime Minister of Australia, "Speech by the Prime Minister: Launch of Statement on the Environment," Wentworth, N.S.W., Australia, July 20, 1989; *Pravda* cited in Yuri Markish, "Soviet Environmental Problems Mount," *CPE Agriculture Report* (Washington, D.C.: USDA, ERS), May/June 1989.

16. Leon Lyles, "Possible Effects of Wind Erosion on Soil Productivity," *Journal of Soil and Water Conservation*, November/December 1975.

17. Walter V.C. Reid, "Sustainable Development: Lessons from Success," *Environment*, May 1989; International Council for Research in Agroforestry (ICRAF)-Nitrogen Fixing Tree Association International Workshop, *Perennial Sesbania Species in Agroforestry Systems* (Nairobi: ICRAF, 1989).

18. Michael E. Bannister and P.K.R. Nair, "Alley Cropping as a Sustainable Agricultural Technology for the Hillsides of Haiti: Experience of an Agroforestry Outreach Project," *American Journal of Alternative Agriculture*, Vol. 5, No. 2, 1990.

19. Paul Kerkhof, *Agroforestry in Africa: A Survey of Project Experience* (London: Panos Publications Ltd, 1990).

20. World Bank, *Vetiver Grass (Vetiveria zizanioides): A Method of Vegetative Soil and Moisture Conservation* (New Delhi: 1987); Sandra Postel, "Halting Land Degradation," in Lester R. Brown et al., *State of the World 1989* (New York: W.W. Norton & Co., 1989).

21. Visit by Sandra Postel, Worldwatch Institute, to two experimental villages and discussions with the Governor of Mizhi County and scientists at the Mizhi Experiment Station, Shaanxi Province, China, June 14 and 15, 1988.

22. USDA, ERS, *Agricultural Resources: Cropland, Water, and Conservation Situation and Outlook Report*, Washington, D.C., September 1990.

23. National Research Council/National Academy of Sciences, *Alternative Agriculture* (Washington, D.C.: National Academy Press, 1989); The President of the Republic of Indonesia, Presidential Instruction No. 3, "Improvement of Control of Brown Planthopper (Wereng Coklat), An Insect Pest of Rice," Jakarta, Indonesia, November 5, 1986.

24. USDA, ERS, *World Grain Database*; James J. MacKenzie and Mohamed T. El-Ashry, *Ill Winds: Airborne Pollution's Toll on Trees and Crops* (Washington, D.C.: World Resources Institute, 1988); Environmental Protection Agency, Environmental Research Laboratory, *The Economic Effects of Ozone on Agriculture* (Washington, D.C.: 1984).

25. Timothy C. Weiskel, Harvard Divinity School, "Cultural Values and Their Environmental Implications: An Essay on Knowledge, Belief, and Global Survival," North American Conference on Religion and Ecology, Washington, D.C., May 15–17, 1990.

CHAPTER 7. A Stable World Population

1. U.S. Department of Energy, Energy Information Administration, *International Energy Annual 1989* (Washington, D.C.: 1991); Population Reference Bureau (PRB), *World Population Data Sheet 1989* (Washington, D.C.: 1989).

2. PRB, *World Population Data Sheet 1991* (Washington, D.C.: 1991); Eduard Bos et al., *Africa Region Population Projections, Asia Region Population Projections, Latin America and the Caribbean Region Population Projections, Europe, Middle East, and North Africa Region Population Projections*, 1990–91 editions, Policy, Research, and External Affairs Working Paper Series (Washington, D.C.: World Bank, 1991).

3. James Brooke, "Feeding on 19th Century Conditions, Cholera Spreads in Latin America," *New York Times*, April 21, 1991; World Bank, *World Development Report 1990* (New York: Oxford University Press: 1990).

4. PRB, *World Population Data Sheet 1991*.

5. U.N. Department of International Economic and Social Affairs (DIESA), *Monthly Bulletin of Statistics*, March 1991; PRB, *World Population Data Sheet 1991*.

6. U.N. DIESA, *Monthly Bulletin of Statistics*; PRB, *World Population Data Sheet 1991*.

7. U.N. Population Fund (UNFPA), *State of World Population 1991* (New York: 1991).

8. PRB, *World Population Data Sheet 1991.*

9. Ibid.

10. Bos et al., *Latin America Region Projections* and *Asia Region Projections.*

11. Bos et al., *Europe Region Projections* and *Africa Region Projections.*

12. Quote from Economic and Social Commission for Asia and the Pacific, *Population of Japan,* Country Monograph Series No. 11 (New York: United Nations, 1984); Carl Haub, PRB, Washington, D.C., private communication, October 17, 1988; Machiko Yanagishita, PRB, Washington, D.C., private communication, May 24, 1991; see also Irene V. Taeuber, *The Population of Japan* (Princeton, N.J.: Princeton University Press, 1958).

13. U.S. Department of Agriculture (USDA), Economic Research Service (ERS), *World Grain Database* (unpublished printouts) (Washington, D.C.: 1990); Population Information Program, "Population and Birth Planning in the People's Republic of China" *Population Reports,* Johns Hopkins University, Baltimore, Md., January/February 1982; Haub, private communication.

14. USDA, ERS, *World Grain Database*; PRB, *World Population Data Sheet 1991.*

15. Jodi L. Jacobson, *Planning the Global Family,* Worldwatch Paper 80 (Washington, D.C.: Worldwatch Institute, December 1987).

16. UNFPA, *State of World Population*; in the 1991 Persian Gulf War, the United States had $44 billion in direct costs such as combat pay, fuel, amunition, etc., according to Marcus Corbin, Center for Defense Information, Washington, D.C., private communication, May 28, 1991.

17. Jodi L. Jacobson, *Women's Reproductive Health: The Silent Emergency,* Worldwatch Paper 102 (Washington, D.C.: Worldwatch Institute, June 1991).

18. Stanley K. Henshaw et al., *Teenage Pregnancy in the United States: The Scope of the Problem and State Responses* (New York: Alan Guttmacher Institute, 1989); Susheela Singh and Deirdre Wulf, *Today's Adolescents, Tomorrow's Parents: A Portrait of the Americas* (New York: Alan Guttmacher Institute, 1990); Center for Population Options, "The Facts: Teenage Pregnancy and Sexually Transmitted Diseases in Latin America," Washington, D.C., August 1990; Center for Population Options, "The Facts: Teenage Pregnancy in Africa," Washington, D.C., September 1990.

19. World Bank, *World Development Report 1984* (New York: Oxford University Press, 1984).

20. World Bank, *World Development Report 1990.*

21. Jodi L. Jacobson, *The Challenge of Survival: Safe Motherhood in the SADCC Region,* Report of the Conference on Safe Motherhood for the Countries of the Southern African Development Coordinating Council, Harare, Zimbabwe, October 29 to November 1, 1990 (Washington, D.C.: World Bank and Family Care International); Government of Tanzania, "Tanzania Status Report on Maternal Health," paper presented at the Conference on Safe Motherhood.

22. Krystyna Chlebowska, *Literacy for Rural Women in the Third World* (Paris: United Nations Educational, Scientific, and Cultural Organization, 1990).

23. For a study of the cost per student of providing primary education in low-income countries, see J.C. Eicher, *Educational Costing and Financing in Developing Countries: Focus on Sub-Saharan Africa,* World Bank Staff Working Paper 655 (Washington, D.C.: World Bank, 1984).

24. Based on William U. Chandler, *Investing in Children,* Worldwatch Paper 64 (Washington, D.C.: Worldwatch Institute, June 1985).

25. UNFPA, *State of World Population.*

26. World Bank, *World Development Report 1984.*

27. Ibid.

28. Ibid.

CHAPTER 8. From Growth to Sustainable Progress

1. For a fuller discussion, see Robin Broad et al., "Development: The Market is Not Enough," *Foreign Policy,* Winter 1990–91.

2. See Jodi L. Jacobson, *Women's Reproductive Health: The Silent Emergency* Worldwatch Paper No. 102 (Washington, D.C.: Worldwatch Institute, June 1991).

3. The $20-trillion dollar world economy is a Worldwatch Institute estimate based on 1988 gross world product from Central Intelligence Agency (CIA), *Handbook of Economic Statistics, 1989* (Washington, D.C.: 1989), with Soviet and Eastern Europe gross national products extrapolated from Paul Marer, *Dollar GNP's of the USSR and Eastern Europe* (Baltimore, Md.: Johns Hopkins University Press, 1985), with adjustments to 1990 based on growth rates from International Monetary Fund (IMF), *World Economic Outlook* (Washington, D.C.: October 1990), and from CIA, *Handbook of Economic Statistics,* with the composite deflator from Office of Management and Budget, *Historical Tables, Budget of the United States Government, Fiscal Year 1990* (Washington, D.C.: U.S. Government Printing Office, 1989); 1900 global

world output from Lester R. Brown and Sandra Postel, "Thresholds of Change," in Lester Brown et al., *State of the World 1987* (New York: W.W. Norton & Co., 1987).

4. See Herman Daly, "Towards an Environmental Macroeconomics," presented at "The Ecological Economics of Sustainability: Making Local and Short-Term Goals Consistent with Global and Long-Term Goals," the International Society for Ecological Economics, Washington, D.C., May 1990; see also Paul R. Ehrlich, "The Limits to Substitution: Meta-Resource Depletion and a New Economic-Ecological Paradigm," *Ecological Economics*, No. 1, 1989.

5. Peter M. Vitousek et al., "Human Appropriation of the Products of Photosynthesis," *BioScience*, June 1986; Population Reference Bureau (PRB), *1990 World Population Data Sheet* (Washington, D.C.: 1990).

6. Department of Energy (DOE), Energy Information Agency (EIA), *State Energy Data Report, Consumption Estimates, 1960–1988* (Washington, D.C.: 1990); DOE, EIA, *Annual Energy Review 1989* (Washington, D.C.: 1990); U.S. Department of Commerce, Bureau of the Census, *Statistical Abstract of the United States 1990* (Washington, D.C.: U.S. Government Printing Office, 1990).

7. Total vehicle kilometers for 1965–70 from U.S. Department of Commerce, *Historical Statistics of the United States, Colonial Times to 1970, Bicentennial Edition* (Washington, D.C., 1975); 1970–88 from DOE, EIA, *Annual Energy Review 1989*.

8. PRB, *1990 World Population Data Sheet*.

9. Alan B. Durning, *Poverty and the Environment: Reversing the Downward Spiral*, Worldwatch Paper 92 (Washington, D.C.: Worldwatch Institute, November 1989).

10. Organisation for Economic Co-operation and Development, *OECD In Figures* (Paris: 1990); Kit D. Farber and Gary L. Rutledge, "Pollution Abatement and Control Expenditures, 1984–87," *Survey of Current Business*, U.S. Department of Commerce, June 1989.

CHAPTER 9. Better Indicators of Human Welfare

1. David Pearce et al., *Blueprint for a Green Economy* (London: Earthscan Publications Ltd, 1989).

2. Robert Repetto, "No Accounting for Pollution: A New Means of Calculating Wealth Can Save the Environment," *Washington Post*, May 28, 1989.

3. Jim MacNeill, "Strategies for Sustainable Economic Development," *Scientific American*, September 1989.

4. U.N. Food and Agriculture Organization, *Forest Products Yearbook 1988* (Rome: 1990).
5. Robert Repetto et al., *Wasting Assets: Natural Resources in the National Income Accounts* (Washington, D.C.: World Resources Institute, 1989).
6. $2.2 billion figure from Michael Weisskopf, "In Plea Bargain, Exxon Accepts Criminal Liability," *Washington Post,* March 14, 1991; James S. Cannon, *The Health Costs of Air Pollution: A Survey of Studies Published 1984–1989* (New York: American Lung Association, 1990).
7. Frank Bracho, "Towards More Effective Development Indicators," in The Caracas Report on Alternative Development Indicators, *Redefining Wealth and Progress: New Ways to Measure Economic, Social and Environmental Change* (New York: The Bootstrap Press, 1989).
8. Garrett Hardin, "Paramount Positions in Ecological Economics," presented at "The Ecological Economics of Sustainability: Making Local and Short-Term Goals Consistent with Global and Long-Term Goals," International Society for Ecological Economics, Washington, D.C., May 1990.
9. Repetto et al., *Wasting Assets*; Ernst Lutz and Mohan Munasinghe, "Accounting for the Environment," *Finance & Development,* March 1991.
10. U.N. Development Programme (UNDP), *Human Development Report 1991* (New York: Oxford University Press, 1991); Herman E. Daly and John B. Cobb, *For the Common Good: Redirecting the Economy Toward Community, The Environment, and a Sustainable Future* (Boston: Beacon Press, 1989).
11. UNDP, *Human Development Report 1991*.
12. Ibid. Note that adjusting per capita GDP for purchasing power gives a better indication of command over resources than unadjusted figures do, and that the two sets of figures can vary greatly. Sri Lanka's adjusted GDP per capita is $2,120, while its unadjusted figure (in 1989 dollars) is $430. Switzerland's adjusted figure is $17,220, compared with an unadjusted figure of $30,270.
13. UNDP, *Human Development Report 1991*.
14. Daly and Cobb, *For the Common Good*.
15. Ibid. Figure 9–1 is based on Clifford W. Cobb and John B. Cobb, Jr., revised Index of Sustainable Economic Development, according to C.W. Cobb, Sacramento, Calif., private communication, September 28, 1990.
16. World Bank, *World Development Report 1990* (New York: Oxford University Press, 1990); U.S. Department of Agriculture, Economic Research Service, *World Grain Database* (unpublished

printouts) (Washington, D.C.: 1990). Based on the authors' personal observations, to avoid starvation a person needs roughly 1 pound of grain per day, while 13 ounces is enough for survival with minimum physical activity.

17. Effects of too high a level of animal fat consumption from Committee on Diet and Health, Food and Nutrition Board, National Research Council, *Diet and Health: Implications for Reducing Chronic Disease Risk* (Washington, D.C.: National Academy Press, 1989).

18. Hazel Henderson, "Moving Beyond Economism: New Indicators for Culturally Specific, Sustainable Development," in Caracas Report on Alternative Development Indicators, *Redefining Wealth and Progress*.

CHAPTER 10. Reshaping Government Incentives

1. Robert Repetto, *Paying the Price: Pesticide Subsidies in Developing Countries* (Washington, D.C.: World Resources Institute, 1985); Egyptian gross domestic product from World Bank, *World Development Report 1990* (New York: Oxford University Press, 1990); Egyptian health spending based on various Egyptian ministry reports provided by the World Bank.

2. Sandra Postel, *Defusing the Toxics Threat: Controlling Pesticides and Industrial Waste*, Worldwatch Paper 79 (Washington, D.C.: Worldwatch Institute, September 1987).

3. See Robert Repetto, *The Forest for the Trees?: Government Policies and the Misuse of Forest Resources* (Washington, D.C.: World Resources Institute, 1988); Robert Repetto, "Deforestation in the Tropics," *Scientific American*, April 1990.

4. Estimate of $500 million to $1 billion from Robert Repetto and Frederik van Bolhuis, *Natural Endowments: Financing Resource Conservation for Development* (Washington, D.C.: World Resources Institute, 1989); 1990 estimate of total Amazon deforestation from Philip M. Fearnside et al., "Deforestation Rate in Brazilian Amazonia," National Secretariat of Science and Technology, August 1990 (for estimate as of August 1989), to which was added estimated burning in 1990 of 1.8 million hectares, as reported in "Deforestation of Amazon Forest Falls Almost 30 Percent in 1990, Official Says," *International Environment Reporter*, March 13, 1991; subsidies discussed in Dennis J. Mahar, "Deforestation in Brazil's Amazon Region: Magnitude, Rate and Causes," in Gunter Schramm and Jeremy J. Warford, eds., *Environmental Management and Economic Development* (Baltimore, Md.: Johns Hopkins University Press, 1989).

5. Fearnside et al., "Deforestation Rate in Brazilian Amazonia"; James Brooke, "Amazon Forest Loss Is Sharply Cut in Brazil," *New York Times*, March 26, 1991; "Deforestation of Amazon Forest Falls Almost 30 Percent in 1990, Official Says"; see also "Brazil: Latest Deforestation Figures," *Nature*, June 28, 1990; for a discussion of satellite data interpretation, see Philip M. Fearnside, "The Rate and Extent of Deforestation in Brazilian Amazonia," *Environmental Conservation*, Autumn 1990; move to reinstate subsidies from Ricardo Arnt, journalist, São Paulo, Brazil, private communication, May 3, 1991; James Brooke, "Brazilian Leader Acts to Protect the Amazon," *New York Times*, June 26, 1991; Ann Devroy, "U.S. Offers Brazil Trade Cooperation," *Washington Post*, June 19, 1991.

6. Repetto, *Paying the Price*; Robert Repetto, *Skimming the Water: Rent-Seeking and the Performance of Public Irrigation Systems* (Washington, D.C.: World Resources Institute, 1986); Repetto, *The Forest for the Trees?*

7. U.S. Department of Agriculture, Economic Research Service, *Agricultural Resources: Cropland, Water and Conservation: Situation and Outlook Report*, Washington, D.C., September 1990.

8. David Moskovitz, *Profits & Progress Through Least-Cost Planning* (Washington, D.C.: National Association of Regulatory Utility Commissioners, 1989).

9. California Public Utilities Commission, "CPUC, Major Utilities Promote Energy Efficiency and Conservation Programs," press release, San Francisco, Calif., August 29, 1990; Elizabeth Kolbert, "Utility's Rates Tied to Saving of Electricity," *New York Times*, September 1, 1990; "NEES to 'Mine' Customers' kWh," *Electrical World*, October 1989; Oregon Public Utility Commission, "PUC Lauds PP&L's Conservation Program as an Oregon 'First'," press release, Salem, Oreg., July 19, 1990; Armond Cohen, Conservation Law Foundation, Boston, Mass., private communication, October 29, 1990.

10. Howard S. Geller, "Electricity Conservation in Brazil: Status Report and Analysis," American Council for an Energy-Efficient Economy, Washington, D.C., August 1990; David A. Wirth, "Climate Chaos," *Foreign Policy*, Spring 1989.

11. Judith Jacobsen, *Promoting Population Stabilization: Incentives for Small Families*, Worldwatch Paper 54 (Washington, D.C.: Worldwatch Institute, June 1983).

12. D.L. Nortman et al., "A Cost Benefit Analysis of Family Planning Program of Mexican Social Security Administration," paper presented at the general conference of the International Union for the Scientific Study of Population, Florence, Italy,

June 5–12, 1985, cited in Jodi L. Jacobson, *Planning the Global Family*, Worldwatch Paper 80 (Washington, D.C.: Worldwatch Institute, December 1987).

13. Overseas Development Council (ODC) and World Wildlife Fund (WWF), *Environmental Challenges to International Trade Policy: A Conference Report* (Washington, D.C.: 1991); International Monetary Fund, *International Financial Statistics* (Washington, D.C.: various years).

14. Information and Media Relations Division, "General Agreement on Tariffs and Trade (GATT): What it Is, What it Does," (Geneva: General Agreement on Tariffs and Trade, 1990); Third World lost income estimate from Paul Shaw, "Rapid Population Growth and Environmental Degradation: Ultimate versus Proximate Factors," *Environmental Conservation*, Autumn 1989; Steven Shrybman, "International Trade and the Environment: An Environmental Assessment of Present GATT Negotiations," *Alternatives*, Vol. 17, No. 2, 1990; Jeffrey J. Schott, "Uruguay Round: What Can Be Achieved," in Jeffrey J. Schott, ed., *Completing the Uruguay Round* (Washington, D.C.: Institute for International Economics, 1990); Dale E. Hathaway, "Agriculture," in ibid.

15. Ann Davison, "Developing Country Concerns," in *IOCU (International Organization of Consumers Unions) Newsletter*, No. 5, 1990; Herman E. Daly and John B. Cobb, *For the Common Good: Redirecting the Economy Toward Community, the Environment, and a Sustainable Future* (Boston: Beacon Press, 1989).

16. ODC and WWF, *Environmental Challenges to International Trade Policy*; Patti Petesch and Stuart K. Tucker, "Global Trade Turns 'Green'," *Journal of Commerce*, March 8, 1991.

17. Stewart Hudson, "Trade, Environment, and the Negotiations on the General Agreement on Tariffs and Trade (GATT)," National Wildlife Federation, Washington, D.C., September 24, 1990; Clyde H. Farnsworth, "Environment Versus Freer Trade," *New York Times*, February 11, 1991.

18. John Hontelez, "The European Single Market: The Economic Cooperation of the 12 EC-Countries and the Possible Environmental Consequences," A Friends of the Earth International Information and Position Paper, 1990; John Elkington, Sustainability, Ltd., London, "1992—The Implications for Industry and the Environment," at Environmental Implications of a Single European Market seminar, IBC Technical Services Ltd., in association with The University of East Anglia, London Press Centre, December 5, 1990; NOAH quote from ibid.

19. Ebba Dohlman, "The Trade Effects of Environmental Regula-

tion," *OECD Observer*, February/March 1990; Court decision from Laurids Mikaelsen, Economic Minister, Embassy of Denmark, Washington, D.C., private communication, May 3, 1991; "*Commission of the European Communities* v. *Kingdom of Denmark*," September 20, 1988, in *Court of Justice of the European Communities, Reports of Cases before the Court, 1988, Vol. 8* (Luxembourg: Office for Official Publications of the European Communities, 1988). Note that some view this decision as only a partial victory, since Denmark was denied the right to require that bottles be officially approved, which makes it difficult to ensure that they are refilled.

20. Robert Reinhold, "Mexico Proclaims an End to Sanctuary for Polluters," *New York Times*, April 18, 1991; "Panels to Vote on Free Trade Issue," *Weekly Bulletin*, Energy and Environmental Study Institute, Washington, D.C., May 13, 1991; John Dillin, "Mexico's Pollution Threatens Free Trade," *Christian Science Monitor*, May 13, 1991.

CHAPTER 11. Green Taxes

1. Air pollution costs from James S. Cannon, *The Health Costs of Air Pollution: A Survey of Studies Published 1984–1989* (New York: American Lung Association, 1990).

2. Louis Harris, Louis Harris & Associates et al., *The Rising Tide: Public Opinion, Policy & Politics* (Washington, D.C.: Americans for the Environment, 1989); also, a poll taken in June 1990 in France found that 61 percent of French citizens were willing to pay more taxes if the proceeds went toward environmental projects, "Eco-Taxes May be Delayed by Commission Opposition," *International Environment Reporter*, February 13, 1991.

3. Allen V. Kneese, *The United States in the 1980s* (Stanford, Calif.: The Hoover Institution, 1980); David Pearce et al., *Blueprint for a Green Economy* (London: Earthscan Publications Ltd., 1989); Lawrence H. Goulder, "Using Carbon Charges to Combat Global Climate Change," Stanford University, Stanford, Calif., December 1990.

4. Organisation for Economic Co-operation and Development, *Economic Instruments for Environmental Protection* (Paris: 1989).

5. U.K example from European Community Commission, "Report of the Working Group of Experts from the Member States on the Use of Economic and Fiscal Instruments in EC Environmental Policy," Brussels, May 1990; CFC figures from U.S. House of Representatives, "Omnibus Budget Reconciliation Act of 1989, Conference Report to Accompany H.R. 3299," Washington,

D.C., November 21, 1989; Joint Committee on Taxation, "Estimated Revenue Effects of Conference Agreement on Revenue Provisions of H.R. 3299," Washington, D.C., November 21, 1989; Michael Weisskopf, "A Clever Solution for Pollution: Taxes," *Washington Post*, December 12, 1989.

6. Estimated tax revenues in Table 11–1 based on U.S. Congressional Budget Office (CBO), *Carbon Charges as a Response to Global Warming: The Effects of Taxing Fossil Fuels* (Washington, D.C.: 1990); hazardous waste estimates are 1985 figures from World Resources Institute, *World Resources 1990–91* (New York: Oxford University Press, 1990); virgin pulp estimate based on 1987 figures in Alice H. Ulrich, *U.S. Timber Production, Trade, Consumption, and Price Statistics 1950–87* (Washington, D.C.: U.S. Department of Agriculture, 1989); pesticide sales are 1988 figures in U.S. Environmental Protection Agency (EPA), *Pesticides Industry Sales and Usage* (Washington, D.C.: February 1990); sulfur dioxide and nitrogen oxide emission estimates are for 1988 in EPA, *National Air Quality Emissions and Trends Report, 1988* (Research Triangle Park, N.C.: 1990); CFC tax exists and revenue estimates for 1994 from U.S. House of Representatives, "Omnibus Budget Reconciliation Act of 1989, Conference Report to Accompany H.R. 3299," and from Joint Committee on Taxation, "Estimated Revenue Effects of Conference Agreement on Revenue Provisions of H.R. 3299"; groundwater depletion estimates are for 1980 in U.S. Geological Survey, *National Water Summary 1983—Hydrologic Events and Issues* (Washington, D.C.: U.S. Government Printing Office, 1983).

7. Dieter Teufel et al., "Ökosteuern als marktwirtschaftliches Instrument im Umweltschutz: Vorschläge für eine ökologische Steuerreform," Umwelt und Prognose Institut, Heidelberg, West Germany, April 1988.

8. Carbon dioxide emissions goals from "Germany and the Greenhouse: A Closer Look," *Global Environmental Change Report*, August 17, 1990, from "East Germany: Country Will Comply with CFC Ordinance of West Germany, Seeks Smaller CO_2 Cut," *International Environment Reporter*, July 1990, from "Japan to Stabilize Greenhouse Gas Emissions by 2000," *Global Environmental Change Report*, July 20, 1990, from "Switzerland to Announce Stabilization Goal at Second World Climate Conference," *Global Environmental Change Report*, July 20, 1990, from "The Netherlands Sets CO_2 Emissions Tax for 1990," *Global Environmental Change Report*, December 22, 1989, from "Country Profiles: Denmark," *European Energy Report*, May 1990, from The Ministry of Environment and Energy, *Action for a Common Future: Swedish National Report for Bergen Conference*, May 1990 (Stock-

holm: 1989), from Michael Weisskopf and William Booth (for
the UK), "U.N. Report Predicts Dire Warming," *Washington
Post*, May 26, 1990, from Gunnrr Mathisen, Secretariate for
Climate Affairs, Ministry of the Environment, Norway, private
communication, January 30, 1990, from "Austria to Reduce
CO_2 Emissions 20% by 2005," *Global Environmental Change
Report*, September 14, 1990, from Emmanuele D'Achon, First
Secretary, Embassy of France, private communication, October
10, 1990, and from Bill Hare, Australian Conservation Foundation, private communication, October 17, 1990; carbon taxes
from Geraldine C. Kay, "Global Climate Change Timeline,"
Global Environmental Change Report, July 28, 1990, from "Nation Adopts Carbon Dioxide Tax; Measure to be Higher on
Coal than Gas," *International Environment Report*, March 1990,
and from Anders Boeryd, Fuel Market Division, National Energy Administration, Sweden, private communication, August
10, 1990; Sweden energy taxes from a translation of the main
proposals of The Swedish Government Bill on Environmental
Policy presented to the Swedish Parliament in February 1991,
and from Ola Jornstedt, "Green Taxes Gaining Ground in Sweden," *enviro*, April 1991.

9. Debora MacKenzie, ". . .as Europe's Ministers Fail to Agree on
Framework for Green Taxes," *New Scientist*, September 29,
1990; the issue of whether to tax energy overall or carbon emissions is currently a matter of debate, David Gardner, "Green
Hopes Rise in a Grey Area," (London) *Financial Times*, May 13,
1991.

10. U.S. House of Representatives, "Omnibus Budget Reconciliation Act of 1989, Conference Report to Accompany H.R.
3299"; Joint Committee on Taxation, "Estimated Revenue Effects of Conference Agreement on Revenue Provisions of H.R.
3299."

11. Kennedy Maize, "Budget Summit Looking at Carbon Tax,"
The Energy Daily, June 1, 1990; CBO, *Carbon Charges as a Response to Global Warming*; income tax receipts from U.S. Department of Commerce, Bureau of the Census, *Statistical Abstract of
the United States 1990* (Washington, D.C.: U.S. Government
Printing Office, 1990).

12. CBO, *Carbon Charges as a Response to Global Warming*.

13. Ibid.; CBO estimates are based on pre-Iraqi invasion oil price
projections.

14. For the late Rajiv Gandhi's proposal for such a Planet Protection Fund, see Linda Starke, *Signs of Hope: Working Towards
Our Common Future* (Oxford: Oxford University Press, 1990).

CHAPTER 12. Banking on the Environment

1. World Bank, *World Debt Tables 1990–1991: External Debt of Developing Countries, Vol. I* (Washington, D.C.:1990).
2. Table 12–1 and current assistance data from Organisation for Economic Co-operation and Development (OECD), *Development Cooperation: Efforts and Policies of the Members of the Development Assistance Committee* (Paris: 1990); World Bank, *World Bank Annual Report 1990* (Washington, D.C.: 1990); Inter-American Development Bank, *Inter-American Development Bank Annual Report 1989* (Washington, D.C.: 1990); Asian Development Bank, *Asian Development Bank Annual Report 1989* (Manilla: 1990); OECD, *OECD In Figures* (Paris: 1990).
3. OECD, *Development Cooperation.*
4. Ibid.; Agency for International Development, *Agency for International Development Fiscal Year 1991 Summary Tables* (Washington, D.C.: 1990); Population Reference Bureau, *1990 World Population Data Sheet* (Washington, D.C.: 1990).
5. OECD, "Memo to Participants on Norwegian Aid," Paris, August 29, 1990; NORAD, "The Scale of Norwegian Development Cooperation," Oslo, 1990.
6. "Sarbanes to Move Foreign Aid Bill," *Weekly Bulletin* (Environmental and Energy Study Institute, Washington, D.C.), June 3, 1991.
7. OECD, *Development Cooperation*; World Bank, *Annual Report 1990*; Inter-American Development Bank, *Annual Report 1989*; Asian Development Bank, *Annual Report 1989.*
8. World Bank, *Annual Report 1990*; Bruce Rich, Environmental Defense Fund, "The Environmental Performance of the Public International Financial Institutions and Other Related Issues," Testimony before the Committee on Appropriations, U.S. Senate, Washington, D.C., July 25, 1990; Stephan Schwartzman, *Bankrolling Disasters: International Development Banks and the Global Environment* (Washington, D.C.: Sierra Club, 1986).
9. Barber B. Conable, President, World Bank, "The World Bank and International Finance Corporation," presented to the World Resources Institute, Washington, D.C., May 5, 1987; World Bank, *The World Bank and the Environment—First Annual Report Fiscal 1990* (Washington, D.C.: 1990).
10. Personnel office, World Bank, private communication, November 1, 1990; World Bank, *The World Bank and the Environment*; Bruce Rich, "The Emperor's New Clothes: The World Bank and Environmental Reform," *World Policy Journal*, Spring 1990.

11. Confidential private communications, World Bank staff, October 1990.

12. Howard Geller, "End-Use Electricity Conservation: Options for Developing Countries," Energy Department Paper No. 32, World Bank, Washington, D.C., 1986; World Bank, *Annual Report 1990*; Rich, "Environmental Performance of the Public International Financial Institutions."

13. Environmental assessment process detailed in World Bank, *The World Bank and the Environment*; Rich, "Environmental Performance of the Public International Financial Institutions."

14. Location of the Environment Department in World Bank, *The World Bank and the Environment*.

15. Confidential private communications, World Bank staff.

16. Mahabub Hossain, *Credit for Alleviation of Rural Poverty: The Grameen Bank in Bangladesh*, Research Report 65 (Washington, D.C.: International Food Policy Research Institute, 1988).

17. NGO Working Group on the World Bank, "Position Paper of the NGO Working Group on the World Bank," Geneva, December 1989.

18. Overseas Development Council, "The Brady Plan: An Interim Assessment," Washington, D.C., 1990; Canadian House of Commons, *Securing Our Global Future: Canada's Stake in the Unfinished Business of Third World Debt*, Minutes of Proceedings and Evidence of the Standing Committee on External Affairs and International Affairs, June 7, 1990; Steven Mufson, "Polish Debt Cut in Half," *Washington Post*, March 16, 1991; Peter Ford, "Egyptian Economy Reaps Rewards of Gulf Stance," *Christian Science Monitor*, May 29, 1991.

19. World Bank, *World Debt Tables 1990–1991*; Canadian House of Commons, *Securing Our Global Future*; Jane Perlez, "U.S. Forgives Loans to 12 African Countries," *New York Times*, January 10, 1990.

20. David E. Rosenbaum, "US Has Received $50 Billion in Pledges for War," *New York Times*, February 11, 1991; Robert Repetto and Frederik van Bolhuis, *Natural Endowments: Financing Resource Conservation for Development* (Washington, D.C.: World Resources Institute, 1989); David Bigman, "A Plan to End LDC Debt and Save the Environment Too," *Challenge*, July/August 1990.

21. Thomas E. Lovejoy, "Aid Debtor Nations' Ecology," *New York Times*, October 4, 1984; Diana Page, "Debt-for-Nature Swaps—Experience Gained, Lessons Learned," *International Environmental Affairs*, January 1990; The Nature Conservancy,

"Officially Sanctioned Debt-for-Nature Swaps to Date," Washington, D.C., January 1991.

22. Rogue Sevilla Larrea and Ulvaro Umaña, "Pour qué Canjear Deuda por Naturaleca," World Wildlife Fund, World Resources Institute, and Nature Conservancy, Washington, D.C., 1989; The White House, "Fact Sheet: American Business and Private Sector Development Initiative for Central and Eastern Europe," March 20, 1991.

23. World Bank, *The World Bank and the Environment*; World Bank, "Funding for the Global Environment," Discussion Paper, Washington, D.C., February 1990; Steven Mufson, "World Bank Wants Fund to Protect Environment," *Washington Post*, May 3, 1990; Letter to Barber Conable, president, World Bank, from David A. Wirth et al., National Resources Defense Council (NRDC), on behalf of NRDC and six other national environmental groups, Washington, D.C., March 9, 1990; "Global Environment Facility Remains an Empty Vessel," *ECO* (newspaper of nongovernmental groups monitoring the climate negotiation meeting in Geneva), June 26, 1991.

24. David Reed, *The Global Environment Facility* (Washington, D.C.: World Wildlife Fund-International, 1991); "New Facility Prepares to Launch First Projects," *World Bank News*, May 9, 1991; funding mechanism as a centerpiece of the Brazil Conference from Mostafa Tolba quoted in Linda Starke, *Signs of Hope: Working Towards Our Common Future* (Oxford: Oxford University Press, 1990).

CHAPTER 13. The Struggle for a New World

1. Alan B. Durning, *Action at the Grassroots: Fighting Poverty and Environmental Decline*, Worldwatch Paper 88 (Washington, D.C.: Worldwatch Institute, January 1989).

2. Alan B. Durning, "People Power and Development," *Foreign Policy*, Fall 1989.

3. Central Intelligence Agency (CIA), *Handbook of Economic Statistics, 1990* (Washington, D.C.: 1990); Robin Broad et al., "Development: The Market is Not Enough," *Foreign Policy*, Winter 1990–91.

4. CIA, *Handbook of Economic Statistics*; James Rush, *The Last Tree: Reclaiming the Environment in Tropical Asia* (New York: The Asia Society, 1991).

5. "Thousands in Brazil Attend Slain Ecologist's Funeral," *Washington Post*, December 26, 1988; Stan Sesser, "A Reporter At Large: Logging the Rain Forest," *New Yorker*, May 27, 1991.

6. Hilary F. French, *Green Revolutions: Environmental Reconstruction*

in *Eastern Europe and the Soviet Union*, Worldwatch Paper 99 (Washington, D.C.: Worldwatch Institute, November 1990).

7. John Ryan, "War and Teaks in Burma," *World Watch*, September/October 1990.

8. "The Environmental Protection Society Malaysia," document presented at "Beyond Boundaries: Issues in Asian and American Environmental Activism," Asia Society, New York, April 25–26, 1991.

9. Steve Askin, "Mobutu Comes Calling," *Africa News*, June 12, 1989.

10. U.N. Development Programme, *Human Development Report 1991* (New York: Oxford University Press, 1991); Steven Mufson, "Study Faults Third World Priorities," *Washington Post*, May 23, 1991.

11. Industry opposition from Center for Strategic and International Studies, "Implications of Global Climate Policies," A Report for the Global Climate Coalition, June 27, 1989.

12. Martha M. Hamilton, "Big Mac Attacks Trash Problem," *Washington Post*, April 17, 1991; Matthew L. Wald, "Two Big California Utilities Plan to Cut CO_2 Emissions," *New York Times*, May 21, 1991.

13. For a more detailed discussion of this time of change, see Charles William Maynes, "America Without the Cold War," *Foreign Policy*, Spring 1990, and Paul H. Nitze, "America: An Honest Broker," and Robert Tucker, "1989 and All That," both in *Foreign Affairs*, Fall 1990.

14. Malcolm W. Browne, "93 Nations Agree to Ban Chemicals That Harm Ozone," *New York Times*, June 30, 1990.

15. Richard Elliot Benedick, *Ozone Diplomacy* (Cambridge, Mass.: Harvard University Press, 1991).

16. Jim Vallette and Heather Spalding, eds., *The International Trade in Wastes: A Greenpeace Inventory* (Washington, D.C.: Greenpeace, 1990); U.N. Office for Ocean Affairs and the Law of the Sea, "Law of the Sea Bulletin," No. 16, December 1990; "Antarctic Treaty Negotiators Agree to 50-Year Ban on Drilling, Mining Activity," *International Environment Reporter*, May 8, 1991.

17. Ken Snyder, "Forest Priorities," *ECO* (newspaper of nongovernmental groups monitoring the climate negotiation meeting in Chantilly, Va.), February 14, 1991; Peter H. Sand, "Air Pollution in Europe: International Policy Responses," *Environment*, December 1987; Ulises Canchola, "Water Diplomacy: A Mexican Agenda for Transboundary Groundwater Negotiations with the United States," *Praxis*, Spring 1991.

18. World Resources Institute, *Greenhouse Warming: Negotiating a*

Global Regime (Washington, D.C., 1991); Michael Weisskopf and William Booth, "In West, U.S. Stands Alone on Warming Issue," *Washington Post*, November 6, 1990.

19. Durwood Zaelke and James Cameron, "Global Warming and Climate Change—An Overview of the International Legal Process," *The American University Journal of International Law and Policy*, Winter 1990; Wu Zongxin and Wei Zhihong, "Energy Consumption and CO_2 Emission in China," Institute of Nuclear Energy Technology, Tsinghua University, Beijing, China, December 1989.

20. Nicola Pain, "Millions Could Become Climate Refugees," *ECO* (newspaper of nongovernmental groups monitoring the climate negotiation meeting in Chantilly, Va.), February 11, 1991.

21. Joyce R. Starr and Daniel C. Stoll, eds., *The Politics of Scarcity: Water in the Middle East* (Boulder, Colo.: Westview Press, 1988); Alan Cowell, "Next Flashpoint in Middle East: Water," *New York Times*, April 16, 1989; Population Reference Bureau, *World Population Data Sheet 1991* (Washington, D.C.: 1991).

22. UNEP's role in ozone accords is recounted in Benedick, *Ozone Diplomacy*.

23. U.N. Department of Public Information, *Everyone's United Nations: A Handbook on the Work of the UN* (New York: 1986); Edward Goldsmith and Nicholas Hildyard, "World Agriculture: Toward 2000—FAO's Plan to Feed the World," *The Ecologist*, March/April 1991; Marcus Colchester and Larry Lohmann, *The Tropical Forestry Action Plan: What Progress?* (Penang, Malaysia: World Rainforest Movement and *The Ecologist*, 1990).

24. UNEP budget from W.R. Prescott, "The Rights of Earth: An Interview with Dr. Noel J. Brown," *In Context*, No. 22; "The National Wildlife Federation," information sheets, Washington, D.C., May 10, 1991.

25. Roy P. Basler, ed., *The Collected Works of Abraham Lincoln*, Vol. 2, 1953, cited in Suzy Platt, ed., *Respectfully Quoted: A Dictionary of Quotations Requested from the Congressional Research Service* (Washington, D.C.: Library of Congress, 1989).

26. Tim Golden, "A Brazil Rain Forest Hunter-Gatherer Takes in the Town," *New York Times*, April 17, 1991.

Index